The Endangered Species Road Trip

the

ENDANGERED

SPECIES

ROAD
TRIP

A Summer's Worth of
DINGY MOTELS, POISON OAK,
RAVENOUS INSECTS,
and the **RAREST SPECIES**
in North America

CAMERON MACDONALD

GREYSTONE BOOKS

Vancouver/Berkeley

Greystone Books Ltd.
343 Railway Street, Suite 201
Vancouver BC V6A 1A4
www.greystonebooks.com

Cataloguing data available from Library and Archives Canada
ISBN 978-1-55365-935-8 (pbk.)
ISBN 978-1-55365-936-5 (epub)

Editing by Nancy Flight
Copy editing by Shirarose Wilensky
Cover and text design by Heather Pringle
Cover illustration by Ryan Heshka
Photographs by Cameron MacDonald and Briana Fraser
Printed and bound in Canada by Friesens
Distributed in the U.S. by Publishers Group West

We gratefully acknowledge the financial support of the Canada Council for the Arts, the British Columbia Arts Council, the Province of British Columbia through the Book Publishing Tax Credit, and the Government of Canada through the Canada Book Fund for our publishing activities.

Greystone Books is committed to reducing the consumption of old-growth forests in the books it publishes. This book is one step toward that goal.

"I have found out that there ain't no surer way to find out whether you like people or hate them than to travel with them." MARK TWAIN, *Tom Sawyer Abroad*

contents

prologue

My first lecture of the semester was a disaster. I wanted to show some pretty pictures of species and landscapes in an attempt to get the students excited about the course, but by the lecture's midpoint my confidence was shot and the embryonic semester promised to be a long one.

It went something like this. Fifteen slides into the lecture was a stunning image of a polar bear that I intended to use to launch into an introductory rant about the effects of climate change on Arctic ecosystems. But before I could rant, a young woman in the front row raised her hand.

"Wow," she asked, "did you take that picture?"

"No," I answered. "I've never seen a polar bear in the wild."

The next image was of an impossibly cute black-footed ferret. Last October, I said, thirty-four black-footed ferrets were reintroduced to Grasslands National Park in southern Saskatchewan, which is truly remarkable, given that in 1986 there were only eighteen of them on the planet. The same young woman raised her hand again: "Did you take that picture?"

"No," I admitted. "It's from the Parks Canada website."

Fearing the next slide, I clicked the projector remote gingerly—northern spotted owl. Because there were only a handful of spotted owls remaining in the wild in British Columbia, I was planning to use this slide to remind the students that the issues we would be discussing were also very local issues. Instead, I mumbled something about having tried, unsuccessfully, to see a spotted owl on several occasions. Trying to see any endangered species is extremely challenging, I explained. They are, after all, proverbial needles in a colossal haystack.

I lingered awkwardly on the spotted owl slide, the laser pointer twitching nervously across the screen. I was pretty sure the next slide was a close-up of a California condor, yet another species I'd only read about. So, instead of clicking the remote and confessing to yet more copyright infringement, I dismissed the class fifteen minutes early. Then, feeling like a charlatan, a cut-and-paste biologist at best, I slunk back to my office, shut the door, and started Googling routes for a road trip that I had first dreamed about several years before.

When I first envisioned the endangered species road trip, I was single and childless. At that time, the notion of driving around the continent and attempting to see a bunch of endangered species seemed like a reasonably straightforward way to spend a working vacation. The plan was to drive from species to species, take some pictures, and generate some firsthand experiences to enliven my rather musty biology lectures.

Now, six years and a thousand students later, the plan hasn't changed, but somehow, between initial vision and looming journey, the vehicle has become much more crowded. Wife, toddler, infant, car seats, strollers, diapers, potty seat, toys, and approximately ninety pop-up books now fill every nook of our newly acquired used minivan. (I must confess I envisioned zooming around the continent in something much less minivan-like.) Even our dog is coming with us because she is way too neurotic to leave with anyone else. The open road is now looking a lot less carefree—Raffi instead of public radio, peanut butter instead of pinot, dirty diapers instead of anything less poopy.

Despite vehicular crowding, I am still committed to the journey, though even the simplest family trip, to Grandma's house or the beach, makes me question the wisdom of this plan. There is good reason to be worried. The route we've picked is long, four months and more than sixteen thousand miles, which is a heck of a long way for a family that doesn't even like to drive. Typically, we only drive about five thousand miles per year, preferring to keep our lives local and simple. Compressing three years of driving into one long road trip will be mentally challenging, physically damaging to backs and bums, and harmful to our eco-friendly personas. Yes, I have fretted about the environmental impact of the journey, about the irony of trying to see endangered species while potentially contributing to their demise through our increased carbon emissions.

There are other problems with this "vacation," too. For starters, my wife, Briana, is a fully urbanized Vancouverite, more comfortable grazing at the local sushi bar than chasing rare woodpeckers through the Everglades. Plus, there are the children—the very young children. Brora, named for the birthplace of her great-grandfather, will be twenty-two months old when we depart, and Finn will be all of seven months old. The farthest we have ever driven with both kids is across town in search of some rare coffee beans, a nightmarish journey during which the kids screamed so loudly that I contemplated driving, kamikaze-like, right into the Pacific. The locations of the endangered species will dictate our route, but the kids will obviously dictate our snail's pace.

But forget those minor problems. The most likely scenario is that I will go wrong. Freak out, scream, sob, abandon ship—all are probable outcomes. I was, at some point in my life, a moderately competent field biologist, but that was more than a decade ago. Now, I am a fulltime biology instructor, plagued by prematurely arthritic knees and a lingering propensity to consume excessive amounts of alcohol. I am a bona fide expert at pasting Googled images into PowerPoint lectures and grading crappy student essays, but do I still possess the necessary skill set to locate a bunch of endangered species with wee children in tow?

Even picking the endangered species to look for on our trip was problematic. Initially, I wanted to try to see all of them, from seaside centipede lichen to blue whale. For British Columbia alone, my initial must-see species list climbed to fourteen species and would have required more than a month of hard driving to try to locate all of them. Clearly, given that we only had four months to complete the entire road trip, I needed to seriously prune the species list if we were going to crisscross the continent. British Columbia would always be there, close at hand, but we likely wouldn't have a chance to explore the swamps of Florida again.

A twinge of regret accompanied the removal of every species deemed superfluous to this trip. In the end, I decided to restrict the list primarily to species that are globally endangered. Many species listed as endangered in British Columbia—the American badger or sage thrasher, for example—are much more common in the United States, where their core ranges are located; Canadian populations constitute the sparse northern fringe of the species ranges, and in Canada, they are rare largely because of geography. This is not to say that retaining viable Canadian populations of these species is not a worthy conservation endeavor, only that such locally threatened species are not facing imminent extinction. Globally threatened species are the more pressing conservation concern because utter extinction is a very probable outcome. I also left on the list a number of other species or subspecies that highlight specific conservation issues or figure prominently in my lectures, which, as mentioned, could benefit from some good stories and bad pictures.

Here's the tentative list of species we hope to see:

1. Vancouver Island marmot (B.C.)
2. Spotted owl (Oregon)
3. California sea otter (Monterey)
4. California condor (Big Sur)
5. Bristlecone pine (Nevada)
6. Desert tortoise (Mojave)
7. Jaguar (Arizona)
8. Sage grouse (Utah)
9. Grizzlies of Yellowstone (Wyoming)
10. Wolves of Yellowstone (Wyoming)
11. Burrowing owl (South Dakota)
12. Black-footed ferret (South Dakota)
13. Kirtland's warbler (Michigan)
14. Wood turtle (Ontario)
15. American chestnut (Ontario)
16. Eastern prickly pear cactus (Ontario)

17. Red-cockaded woodpecker (Georgia)
18. Ivory-billed woodpecker (Florida Panhandle)
19. West Indian manatee (Florida)
20. Florida scrub jay (central Florida)
21. Florida panther (Everglades)
22. Snail kite (Florida)
23. Wood stork (Florida)
24. Piping plover (Cape Cod)
25. Atlantic cod (Maine)
26. Atlantic right whale (Bay of Fundy)
27. Basking shark (Bay of Fundy)
28. Beluga (Quebec)
29. Karner blue butterfly (New York)
30. Plains bison (Saskatchewan)
31. Swift fox (Saskatchewan)
32. Whooping crane (Saskatchewan)
33. Killer whales (back home in B.C.!)
34. Polar bears (on a separate trip to Churchill, Manitoba)

The list includes many of the most endangered species north of the Mexican border. A strength of the list is that it will allow us to cover a great deal of geography, meaning that we will see not only endangered species but also much of the continent. A weakness of the list is that it concentrates on mammals and birds and largely, but not completely, ignores less charismatic taxa—fish, invertebrates, and plants. This is a reality not only of our road trip but of endangered species protection in general; humans tend to be more interested in the plight of charismatic megafauna—jaguars and polar bears—than they are in endangered mollusks or mosses. Our hope is that we can use our megafauna trip as the World Wildlife Fund uses the panda—to highlight issues relevant to all species.

We know that some of these species will be impossible to see—the ivory-billed woodpecker, jaguar, and Florida panther top this list. Ivory-billed woodpeckers were thought to be extinct by the 1940s, but recent, albeit controversial, sightings leave a faint hope that a few persist. The last, lonely wild jaguar in the United States was euthanized in 2009, and recolonization from Mexican populations is now deemed unlikely because of the new border fence. Florida panthers, which are actually an isolated population of mountain lions/cougars, are so scarce and so elusive that it will take a miracle to see one. So we will look for these species, not because we think we will actually see them but rather because we find the idea of trying to see them oddly alluring.

We saw the first species on our list, the Vancouver Island marmot (*Marmota vancouverensis*), on a trial run designed to test our mettle for the actual road trip the following summer. Briana suggested the marmot trip, but I was hesitant—she was eight months pregnant with our second child, a bomb ready to explode. Despite a soggy forecast and a gigantic lineup for the ferry, we made it to a campsite without too much fuss. Traveling with one young kid, it turns out, is about ten times easier than traveling with two. Then, the very next morning, we were able to view and photograph several marmots. Despite being one of the rarest mammals on the planet, they are relatively easy to spot on the ski slopes of Mount Washington near Comox, where the managed slopes mimic the alpine meadows the marmots would typically occupy. It took only an hour's stroll from the ski

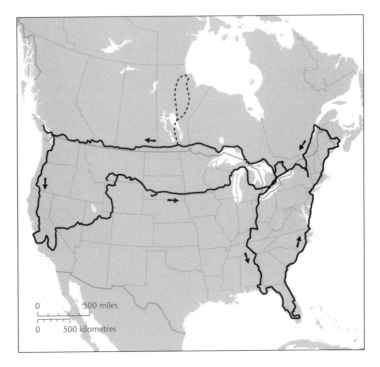

Our route

lodge parking lot to locate our first marmot, which was clearly used to a lot of human activity because even Brora's squealing didn't send it running for its burrow. Then, from a perfect picnic perch, we were able to watch through our binoculars as a female marmot and two curious pups munched wildflowers.

Returning home from our marmot road trip, Briana and I were just starting to plan the route for the real road trip when our son, Finn, was born in mid-October, two weeks late and by way of an emergency c-section. Not surprisingly, the next three months were a blur of dirty diapers, sleepless nights, and botched lectures. All thoughts of road tripping retreated into the recesses of our minds.

It wasn't until February that thoughts of the road trip resurfaced. I came home from work to find Briana leafing through a stack of maps that she and the kids had acquired from the Auto Club. We spent the next several evenings running our fingers along squiggly coastal highways and dead-straight prairie roads, a pastime that roused dreams of prairie skies and mountain passes, country diners and dilapidated motels. Google maps might be useful on occasion, but they are not the real thing, not the medium that will cause anyone to close their eyes and dream of being on the road. I spread all of these maps, state and provincial, across the basement floor, taping them together at their edges to form one massive route planner. Then I highlighted our tentative route with a piece of yarn. The continent made for intimidating wall-to-wall carpeting; the route seemed impossibly long. Standing on British Columbia, Florida was twenty feet away, curling up the far wall. Briana ventured downstairs for a peek, and we shuffled out to the middle of the continent and looked down on the route like orbiting satellites. "We'll never make it," she said.

ONE

where have
THE OWLS GONE?

"To keep every cog and wheel is the first precaution
of intelligent tinkering."
ALDO LEOPOLD, *A Sand County Almanac*

If the first day is indicative of the journey, it's going to be one very long road trip. We leave on May 5, just as gasoline prices are peaking at around $1.40 per liter—the line of credit is going to take a hell of a beating on this trip. Then, despite rising at 4 AM to pack the minivan, we leave two hours later than expected—it takes that long to stuff all of our junk into our newly acquired used minivan. Next, we spend two and a half hours waiting to cross the border into Washington State, the kids howling like coyotes the entire time. We eat a late lunch in a café in Bellingham, less than forty miles south of our house. At this pace, I think to myself, we'll be on the road for the rest of our lives. Halfway through lunch, Brora, who is not yet two years old, has a food-tossing tantrum that causes every other patron to look our way. Leaving Briana with Finn, who is now seven months old, I carry Brora outside. It is pouring rain, real West Coast buckets.

We hit Seattle at rush hour and spend three hours screaming our way down the rain-slick 15 at four miles per hour. We get off in Olympia and start looking for a motel. Our intention is to camp most nights, but the rain is relentless. It turns out there is a conference in town, so it is seemingly impossible to find a pet-friendly motel with vacancies.

Finally, farther south on the 15, we find something within our budget. The room looks exactly like every other crappy motel room—floral bedspread and overbleached sheets, someone's stubble ringing the bathtub, and dark stains on the carpet (blood, I assume). The smell is a mixture of air freshener and pesticides, stale urine and damp mustiness. The room has only one saggy double bed, and it looks like it has seen more action than a D-Day beach. When it is time for bed, Briana and I each take an outside edge and the kids, who have surprisingly sharp elbows, take the middle. Adie, the pooch, reluctantly takes the floor.

I wake in the middle of the night and lie there listening to the rumble of the trucks on the 15, a river of consumption continually flowing north and south. I sit up and watch everyone sleeping in the neon glow of the motel sign. Briana is hanging halfway out of the crappy bed, the two kids are pressed to her back like leeches, and Adie is sleeping on her feet.

After a night of not sleeping, I get up before dawn and try to brew an in-room coffee, which is terrible—already I miss my burr grinder and exotic beans. Dumping out the "coffee," I leash up the wiggling pooch for her morning stroll. Behind the motel is a scrubby patch of forest, and we sniff our way through it, tree to tree. According to Google Maps, we are exactly 189 miles south of our house—why did it take us ten hours to get here?—so it isn't surprising that the forest is very similar to the one we walk through at home, red alder, western red cedar, and Douglas-fir hogging the canopy.

The birds are also similar—spotted towhee, black-capped chickadee, and song sparrow—but then I hear something new. A jay is calling, but it's not the Steller's jay of my backyard; it's a western scrub jay, a species that birders would describe as an accidental in British Columbia. Only a month before departing on the road trip, I found a western scrub jay in a Vancouver neighborhood, where it had been hanging out for the entire winter. But here, in Olympia, scrub jays are common enough that this morning's sighting doesn't justify a phone call to the local rare bird alert.

Twenty years ago, however, a scrub jay sighting in Olympia would have been perhaps as uncommon as Vancouver sightings are today. Like a number of species, scrub jays are currently expanding their range northward, primarily because of habitat modification as the dense temperate rain forest has been logged and replaced with the more open habitat that the scrub jays prefer. Climate change and backyard bird feeders are probably important factors also. I've been thinking a lot about species' ranges lately, why one species' range might shrink to a dot and eventually disappear, whereas another species' range expands to cover much of the continent. I imagine it won't be long before there's a breeding record for scrub jays in British Columbia, and when that happens, what will it mean from a conservation perspective? Will the province embrace its arrival or banish it as an unwanted exotic?

We spend our second day on the road trying to find our traveling pace. Drive for an hour, get out and run around, drive for an hour, stop for lunch, drive for an hour, get out and run around, drive for an hour, stop for the night. Today we manage 225 miles before the screaming forces us to stop in rainy Eugene, Oregon. I wake in the middle of the night and again lie there listening to the rumble of the trucks on the I5. Then I start thinking about northern spotted owls. Tomorrow, in Roseburg, Oregon, I hope to finally see one. I've looked for one in British Columbia several times, but now they are impossible to find because only a few breeding pairs, at best, are left in the entire province. But in Oregon, the critically endangered owls are still numerous enough that my chances of seeing one are better, particularly because I was able to convince a local biologist to help. Finally, I fall back to sleep with visions of owls fluttering in my head.

I can tell Janice Reid, who has worked for the U.S. Forest Service for almost two decades, is a field biologist and not an armchair biologist by the way she walks through the forest. The undergrowth is dense, the forest floor is banana-slug slippery, and the slopes are West Coast steep—and still she proceeds toward the spotted owl nest site without a lick of effort, following an unseen trail without the aid of GPS or compass, miraculously spotting feathers and owl pellets. I used to walk like that, I think to myself as I trundle along behind, gasping on the up slopes and falling on my arse on the way down.

"Are you okay?" Janice asks politely when I take my most obvious tumble.

"Just checking out the undergrowth," I say, removing a stick impaled in my palm.

"Watch out for the poison oak," she says. "It's everywhere." Thank God Briana decided that she and the kids would enjoy spending the day wallowing in the motel pool more than chasing spotted owls through the temperate rain forest.

We are approximately ten miles west of Roseburg, Oregon, which is about two-thirds of the way down Oregon on the 15, and although we are now almost five hundred miles south of Vancouver, the habitat is still similar—except for the poison oak. In Janice's 4×4, we have driven through a series of rather nasty clear-cuts, climbing eventually into a remaining patch of mature forest. In this patch, there is a spotted owl nest that was still active the last time Janice checked on it a couple of weeks ago. But nests have been failing all across Oregon, probably because of the extremely wet spring that has gripped the whole coast.

"We've never seen anything quite like it," she says. "Some years we monitor close to fifty nests in our study area, but this year we've only had four active nests. It's the same story everywhere in Oregon."

Janice's pace slows as we approach the nest site. She points to an inconspicuous broken-topped Douglas-fir.

"The nest is in the cavity at the top." Then she points to whitewash streaking a nearby tree. "The male sometimes perches there."

While she circles around the nest tree, I hang back with my camera at the ready. When no owl appears after five minutes, she reaches into her backpack and pulls out a small cage with a few lab mice in it.

"An enticement to help with the monitoring," she says, placing one squeaking mouse on a nearby branch—a cotton ball ready for harvest.

We circle away, leaving the little mouse to its fate. Ten minutes pass, Janice clucks and hoots, and the mouse continues to scurry back and forth on its branch. Still no owls appear.

"They might have abandoned the nest," Janice says, disappointed, "but hopefully they just aren't hungry and are sleeping the day away. I'll have to check back in a few days."

We return the lucky mouse to the cage and hike back to the truck. Janice writes in her data book and consults a map. "There's another nest not too far from here. The owls are real old-timers. They've produced young every year for a decade."

"Do they mate for life?" I ask.

"More or less," she says.

We drive toward the second nest on a series of logging roads that lies across the landscape like a cobweb. At a particularly narrow spot, a logging truck bombs past us with some big fir logs strapped to its trailer. "There goes the spotted owl habitat," Janice says, laughing the half laugh of someone who has seen a lot of good habitat trucked out.

Habitat loss is still arguably the most serious threat to the spotted owl. Throughout the owl's range, from northern California to southern British Columbia, more than 70 percent of the owl's historical habitat has been logged, and most of the patches of mature forest that remain are, well, patches. Spotted owls are so dependent on mature forest that they are referred to as indicator species of that habitat type, meaning that if you happen upon a spotted owl, you are almost certainly in a large, healthy expanse of old-growth forest. When indicator species, such as spotted owls, disappear from an ecosystem, it is likely to be an early indication that the ecosystem is not functioning properly and that other species will begin to disappear also.

Like canaries in the coal mine, are spotted owls raising the alarm about changes that will soon doom others?

Before we reach the next nest site, we stop at a location where a field assistant recently heard a spotted owl. We walk into the forest, which is even scrappier than the first patch—the trees are younger and the clear-cuts are closer. Janice hoots into the canopy, and then we wait quietly, hoping for a reply.

"There used to be a nest near here every year," Janice whispers, "but then the barred owls moved in and the spotties moved out." Janice hoots again, but the forest only drips in reply.

Back in the truck, Janice shows me where we are on the satellite map.

"Here's the first nest site," she says, pointing to a red sticker, "and here's the nest we're heading towards."

The satellite map clearly illustrates how extensively the landscape has been modified—it is a patchwork quilt of clear-cuts, young plantations, and older remnants. Then she points at the map again. "The stickers with the frowny faces are barred owl nests."

I don't need to count them to know that the frowny stickers significantly outnumber the red stickers.

Barred owls, which are close relatives to spotted owls, are native to the eastern half of North America. However, for reasons that are unclear, they have been expanding their range westward into the traditional territory of the spotted owl. The first barred owl was documented in British Columbia in 1943, and before long, the species moved into Washington and Oregon. Now, they are, along with habitat loss, the most serious threat facing the spotted owl.

Barred owls are more aggressive than spotted owls. They can outcompete, kill and eat, and even sometimes interbreed with spotted owls. Instead of being indicator species of a particular habitat type, they are adaptable habitat generalists—I've seen and heard them in all kinds of habitats, from my urban backyard to remote boreal forest. In Vancouver, they are well known for swooping at joggers in a couple of urban parks.

The arrival of barred owls on the West Coast has greatly complicated the conservation of spotted owls. The most obvious solution is to kill the invading barred owls, but many people, including some who have campaigned hard to save spotted owl habitat in the past, are uncomfortable with such a drastic solution. One concern is that the expansion of the barred owls' range might be entirely natural, a by-product of the birds' remarkable adaptability. Others argue that the expansion of their range is a result of human interference—would the owls have been able to move into temperate rain forests if we humans hadn't first chopped them up? This is an important question, and illuminating data are lacking. Regardless of the answer, though, it is still going to be difficult, physically and ethically, to shoot the thousands of barred owls that now occupy the range of the spotted owl. I don't know if we should be killing barred owls en masse to save spotted owls, and I'm glad it's not my decision to make.

We get out of the truck and hike toward the second nest, which is straight up another steep slope. As we approach the nest, a couple of red-tailed hawks—potential owl predators—are circling low overhead. Janice swears under her breath. Again, I have to wonder: Would these hawks be anywhere near here if this patch of old growth weren't surrounded by clear-cuts?

It takes only ten minutes to reach this nest, which is again in a broken-topped Douglas-fir of relatively modest girth. Once the hawks are long gone, Janice moves farther up the slope to look for a roosting owl and I keep my eye on the nest tree. I see the owl first. It pops its head out of the nest cavity and quickly looks around before tucking back in. I almost squeal with excitement—it had been a long day, and I was really starting to think that we weren't going to see one.

I flag down Janice with some frantic waving and pointing. She makes her way back down to where I am.

"One stuck its head out of the nest," I say.

"She's probably still sitting on eggs," Janice whispers, "but the eggs should be hatching soon."

"How many eggs do they normally lay?"

"Two or three, typically. The female does most of the incubating, and the male does most of the hunting until the young fledge. Mortality is highest for recently fledged juveniles," she says, and as she says it, the female sticks its head out of the nest again and looks right at us.

"Well, now that we've disturbed them, we might as well give them a few calories," she says, with the calm of someone who has seen a lot of spotted owls. Then she reaches into her backpack for a mouse, and before she even has the mouse out of the pack, the male owl flies in and perches on a branch about fifty feet away (because both sexes are identical in plumage, I rely entirely on Janice to differentiate the sexes, which she does, based on their behavior).

"He knows the routine," Janice says, "so get your camera ready."

I have two cameras with me, one with a 400mm telephoto lens and one with an all-purpose 18–105mm lens, and I grab the camera with the telephoto lens. Then Janice places the mouse on a branch only a few yards away. The mouse is out of

Janice's hand for a nanosecond before the owl swoops down, silently, and grabs it.

Of course, I completely miss the desired owl-in-flight shot—it happened so fast and I chose the wrong camera. But it's no big deal, because I am able to rattle off a hundred shots of the male taking the mouse over to the female, who is now also out of the nest, and giving it to her for dinner. Then I sit back and just watch the owls in their habitat—a truly unique and wonderful West Coast experience. The female returns to the nest after a few minutes, while the male perches nearby and watches us with his dark eyes until we depart a few minutes later.

Spotted owl

That evening over dinner, I gush about the owls. I have seen a lot of barred owls, and given that the genetic distance between the two species is slight, I was expecting the spotted owls to look and behave like barred owls with spots. But they were different—shy yet inquisitive cousins, seemingly more solemn than the often boisterous barred, as if they were somehow aware of their bleak future.

In British Columbia, some of the very last spotted owls in the wild were recently captured and brought into a captive breeding program. The hope is that the captive population will quickly grow to the point where captive-born individuals can be reintroduced into the wild. But the provincial biologists seem to have forgotten that a successful reintroduction also requires the availability of high-quality habitat—one cannot release spotted owls into clear-cuts and expect success. Spotted owls require mature forest—and lots of it; the average home range size of a pair of spotted owls in this part of Oregon is typically a couple thousand acres and in British Columbia a territory is probably much larger.

Nevertheless, the habitat at the nest sites we visited was not particularly pristine. Both sites were surrounded by clear-cuts and almost within sight of logging roads. I had expected to reach the nests only after long hikes through untouched old growth. There is a lot of habitat of similar quality in British Columbia, but because the province constitutes the sparse northern fringe of the spotted owls' range, the habitat there must be of better quality if we also hope to save some Canadian "spotties." Conservation efforts on the fringes of a species' range are almost always more challenging than those near the core of the range.

In preparation for my spotted owl search, I had browsed a lot of scientific papers, but the sterile language and complicated figures did not adequately prepare me for how my encounter with the owls would make me feel. Seeing the spotted owls made me feel better about the whole road trip—there really is something special about seeing these species in their habitats.

TWO

flight of
THE PHOENIX

"A journey is like marriage. The certain
way to be wrong is to think you control it."
JOHN STEINBECK, *Travels with Charley:
In Search of America*

I feel energized after seeing the spotted owls—even with a spotted owl biologist for company, I thought my chances of seeing one were fifty-fifty at best. Mood altered by owls, I find myself humming as we drive south, whistling while changing nasty diapers and singing the four children's songs I know in a continuous loop. Then, in northern California, the serotonin wears off and I have my first childlike temper tantrum of the trip.

That morning, the woman at the motel in Roseburg told me that it was about two hours to the California border. But somehow it takes us six hours—for one reason or another, we have to stop at every rest area.

"Finny has a dirty diaper," Briana says.

"Milk," Brora says.

"Is it time for lunch?" Briana asks.

"Out!" screams Brora.

"Wahwahwah!" cries Finn.

"Brora has a dirty diaper," Briana says.

With each stop, my smile gets a little tighter, the singing a little more forced, and my pedal foot a little itchier.

By the time we cross into California—there is actually a manned border crossing at the California-Oregon border, where a very serious Hispanic woman grills us about any fruit we might be smuggling—the shadows are lengthening.

"We'll need to stop soon if we want to camp," Briana says.

"Look at the map and pick a spot," I say.

"Where'd you put the California map?" Briana asks. "Glove box? Nope. Under your seat? Nope. Center console? Nope. Glove box? Nope."

"Well, I put it right there somewhere," I say.

"Where?"

"For Christ's sake," I mutter to myself and then pull off the highway at the next exit.

First, I re-search all the places Briana has already searched. Then, I search backseats and under floor mats. Then, finally, I start throwing every possession we have out of the van's tailgate. The van is packed from floor to ceiling, so there is a lot of crap to throw. Somewhere in the back of my mind, I know that we don't need the map, but I can't let it go until physical exhaustion forces me to take a break. I sit, huffing, on the cooler and look at all the shit scattered about. Then I start methodically reloading.

We never did find that goddamn map.

The whole ridiculous incident reminds me of when my roommate at university was dumped by his girlfriend and then proceeded to throw all of her belongings out of his bedroom window. I remember opening the front door and watching panties and socks float down to the street like giant snowflakes, while the CDs and books came crashing down like meteors.

Back on the road, we pass Mount Shasta, which dominates the landscape at 14,179 feet. Then we start losing elevation, and as we do so, we watch the temperature climb on the van's built-in thermometer. On the flanks of Mount Shasta, the temperature was a bone-chilling thirty-eight degrees Fahrenheit, but by the time we reach the shores of Lake Shasta, the largest reservoir in California, the air temperature is sixty-five degrees Fahrenheit—perfect for camping.

Even without the map, we find a lovely campsite, dominated by widely spaced ponderosa pines, and I take the presence of these stately trees to mean that we have finally crossed into a different biome, which is loosely defined as a large region that shares similar climax vegetation because of similarities in geography and climate. From Vancouver to Roseburg, we had traveled entirely within the Pacific temperate rain forest biome. This meant that, despite being separated by almost 500 miles, the mature forests surrounding Roseburg and Vancouver have a remarkably similar feel. In contrast, Roseburg and tonight's campsite are separated by only 220 miles, but the forest is obviously different—different species, different structure, different feel. Somewhere on the slopes of Mount Shasta, we crossed into the Mediterranean California biome, and we are very happy to be here—it has rained nonstop since we left soggy Vancouver, but suddenly we are witness to a beautiful sunset.

We set up camp quickly, cook a simple spaghetti dinner, and then go for a walk. Whatever grumpiness had gripped me before is gone, alleviated by the smell of the ponderosas and the sound of the western tanagers singing overhead. Despite the perfect weather, we are the only campers other than the campsite hosts—I guess early May is still off-season in these parts—and it is great to watch Adie and Brora run wild around the empty campsite.

Back at the tent, we roll out our most extravagant purchase for the trip—a pair of $120 self-inflating camp mattresses that are as thick as pastrami sandwiches and promise the comfort of a feather bed. We strap the two mattresses together and cover them with real cotton sheets; the queen-sized bottom sheet fits like a glove. Then all four of us crawl under the wool duvet. It feels exactly like sleeping at home, where, despite my initial protests against sharing the bed with our kids, I now need to feel their warm skin and hear their light breathing to fall asleep.

In the middle of the night, Briana and I wake to the sound of a train in the distance. We lie there listening as it approaches, whistle blaring. When the train crosses the nearby trestle bridge, the rails clank madly and the brakes screech wildly, angry sounds that reverberate down the lake in great Doppler waves—it sounds like the engineers have lost control and the train will soon derail right into our campsite. Encircled by Mom, Dad, and dog, the kids sleep through the furor without missing a breath.

A few days later, we are camping on the top of Fremont Peak, which overlooks Monterey Bay to the west and the Salinas Valley to the east. The little state park is perfect—twenty-two campsites scattered throughout oak savannah, a tidy vault toilet, great views in every direction from the 3,097-foot peak, and completely empty except for an elderly couple in a well-maintained Westfalia. Even the town at the bottom of the access road, San Juan Bautista, which was originally a Spanish mission town, is lovely.

Our current plan is to stay here for several days and use our campsite as a base from which to look for both California sea otters and California condors. Plus, we hope to squeeze in side trips to the Monterey Bay Aquarium and the National Steinbeck Center. We use our first full day to get our bearings, driving into Monterey and then down the coast to Big Sur. It is all new to me—the farthest down the coast I had previously driven was San Francisco—and I soak in the scenery along Highway 1, which skirts the Pacific coast through much of California.

Although I needed professional help to find a spotted owl, my intent from the outset has been to try to find most of the endangered species on the list on my own. Before our departure, my research indicated that the most likely spot to see a condor was at the various highway pullouts overlooking the Pacific south of Big Sur. So this is where we head, stopping first at Julia Pfeiffer Burns State Park, which offers a mix of spectacular coastline, scenic waterfalls, and giant redwoods. There, we eat a lunch of bread, tomatoes, and avocado—all the while scanning the skies for the giant silhouette of a condor.

California condors (*Gymnogyps californianus*) are huge birds. They have the greatest wingspan of any bird in North America, almost ten feet on large individuals; they are also perhaps the heaviest, at up to twenty-nine pounds. Given a decent sighting, they are unmistakable—very large black birds with white markings under the wings and a bald head that is orangish in adults and blackish in juveniles. There is some dispute about their evolutionary history, but the most recent evidence suggests that they are one of seven New World vultures in the order Cathartidae, making them distant relatives of hawks and falcons. Surprisingly, the New World vultures are not closely related to the look-alike Old World vultures. These two groups share similarities in appearance not because they are closely related but rather because they fill a similar ecological role in different regions and have thus converged on a similar appearance over millennia, a process known as convergent evolution.

Aside from being the largest bird in North America, the California condor is also one of the most endangered animals in the world. It is likely that condor numbers have been in decline for more than ten thousand years—ever since the continent's megafauna started to disappear as a result of changing climate and the arrival of *Homo sapiens*. By the time of European contact, condors were probably not especially numerous, though they were certainly more widespread—Lewis and Clark observed and shot some condors at the mouth of the Columbia River, which forms the boundary between Washington State and Oregon.

Condors were in serious trouble by the 1950s. Despite intensive management, populations continued to decline as a result of poaching, contact with electric power lines, lead poisoning, and habitat destruction. In 1987, when the last wild condor was captured and incorporated into a captive breeding program, there were only twenty-two condors alive in the world and extinction seemed unavoidable.

Today, condors are still in real trouble. Scattered between a few isolated populations, there are now about 175 individuals in the wild. All of these populations, however, rely on the continual release of individuals from the captive breeding program to sustain their numbers. Only a few condors have nested in the wild, only a few young have successfully fledged, and none of these fledglings have survived to maturity. Clearly, without intensive management, the condors will soon go the way of the dodo. The hope is for self-sustaining condor populations, but that reality is still a long way off.

So there we are, eating our sandwiches and looking for a very rare bird—the condor population around Big Sur numbers about fifty individuals, and they range widely, along the coast and inland to Soledad. The possibility of seeing a condor is complicated by the fact that there are hundreds of turkey vultures in the area. Turkey vultures are another species of New World vulture, and although not huge like the condor, they are large birds with almost six-foot wingspans. Every few minutes, a soaring speck on the horizon gets my heart racing—is it a condor? But sadly no. Each speck as it comes closer materializes into the distinctive V-shaped silhouette of yet another turkey vulture.

After lunch, we spend a few hours playing with the kids in a grassy area overlooking a waterfall that plunges into the cerulean Pacific. Briana and I are constantly reaching for our binoculars to verify that a distant vulture is just that. Brora is busy looking, too.

"Big bird," she says, pointing.

"That's a crow," I say. "The bird we're looking for is even bigger."

"Big bird," she says, pointing to something rustling in the bushes.

"Cool," I say, grabbing the camera. "Lazuli bunting!"

We leave Julia Pfeiffer Burns State Park and drive south on Highway 1, eyes twitching between hairpin curves and blue skies, stopping at every pullout to scan the horizon. The winding road lulls both kids to sleep, making the drive south an enjoyable adult adventure. We drive all the way past Lucia, where a mudslide has kept the highway closed for more than a month and promises to complicate the looming tourist season. Then we drive back north, repeating the pattern of stopping at every pullout.

We are parked in a pullout about five miles south of Big Sur when both kids wake up screaming. It is dinnertime: we need food and shelter; we need our campsite. But I am also tracking a distant speck with my binoculars that might not be a turkey vulture. It's too big, I think to myself. It's too flat. Then, just as the screaming emanating from the backseat reaches a new high point for the trip, the bird turns back south and I get a good look at the silhouette.

"Condor!" I shout. "Condor!"

I struggle to get a better look with the spotting scope, but by the time I line up the scope, the bird has disappeared behind the rocky headland. I want to drive back south in pursuit of this bird, but the van is practically vibrating—even Adie is howling. Swearing under my breath, I pack up the spotting scope and climb into the driver's seat.

"Did you get a good look?" Briana asks, waving a dirty diaper in my general direction.

"Tomorrow," I say. "We'll get a good look tomorrow."

The next morning dawns drizzly and cold, near freezing at 2,500 feet. I walk Adie up to the top of Fremont Peak, and the view, or lack of view, confirms that the clouds are really socked in. Back at the campsite, I crawl into the tent and snuggle under the duvet—there is no reason to rush this morning. "It's a good aquarium day," I say to the still-sleeping Briana.

After the aquarium, which is both impressive and remarkably busy, we again drive south on Highway 1 to look for condors. It is a good way to spend naptime. Again, we stop at every pullout between Big Sur and Julia Pfeiffer Burns State Park, and we go through the motions of getting out and scanning the gray with our binoculars. But it simply is not a condor kind of day. Condors need strong thermals to facilitate soaring, and on days like today, with constant drizzle and patchy fog, they will hunker down and wait for clearer skies. Even the turkey vultures are hiding. Given that condors can eat more than two pounds of carrion at one meal, they can easily go without feeding for several days.

The kids are still sleeping—the aquarium really wore them out—so we decide to start our search for the California sea otter (*Enhydra lutris nereis*). In truth, I was so excited to see a condor that the sea otter has become more of an afterthought—seeing otters on this trip is also less pressing because I have previously seen northern sea otters, a very closely related subspecies, on kayak trips in British Columbia. But we try to see the local otters nonetheless, driving north of Monterey and stopping to scan the various estuaries.

Sea otters (*Enhydra lutris*), at up to one hundred pounds, are the largest members of the weasel family but the smallest of marine mammals. They are a species of the northern Pacific, ranging in a great arc from northern Japan all the way to the tip of Baja—at least that was their historical range. The otter was first scientifically described in 1751 by the naturalist Georg Steller, who also described the Steller's jay, the Steller's sea lion, and the now-extinct Steller's sea cow, among many other species. The sea otter quickly gained a reputation for having the most luxurious fur of any mammal on the planet, an unfortunate reputation to have at a time when pelts were in high demand. Commercial hunting began soon after Steller's description, and thanks to typical human efficiency, the sea otter was nearly extinct throughout its entire range by 1900. More than a million pelts were taken.

The demise of the sea otter had dramatic impacts on intertidal and subtidal ecosystems. Because they need a lot of calories to maintain their body temperature, sea otters are voracious predators of intertidal animals such as mussels, crabs, abalone, and, especially, sea urchins. When sea otters are removed from an area, sea urchins typically proliferate to the point of overabundance. This spiny army runs roughshod over the kelp, munching holdfasts and stipes and quickly replacing biologically diverse kelp forests with urchin barrens—an area with lots of urchins but not much else. So many species are dependent on kelp forests, from juvenile salmon to herbivorous snails, that the loss of kelp forests from an area has a profound, detrimental impact on local biodiversity. The far-reaching effects of removing sea otters make them a textbook example of a keystone species, a species that has greater influence on the ecosystem than would be predicted given their abundance. Remove the keystone from an arch, and the arch collapses; remove a keystone species from an ecosystem, and the ecosystem collapses.

Since sea otters are a keystone species, it is fortunate that we did not harvest the last of them into oblivion. In a moment of wise foresight, the international community banned the harvest of sea otters in 1911, when there were perhaps only a thousand individuals left on the planet, almost all located in the remote Aleutians. Other otter populations were tiny and isolated, and they slowly disappeared. For example, despite protection, the last sea otter in British Columbia was shot in 1929. But the Aleutian populations persisted, and eventually surplus individuals were used for reintroductions in British Columbia, Washington, and Oregon.

The California sea otters, however, descend not from reintroduced Aleutian otters but from a population of about fifty otters that miraculously survived decades of commercial hunting in the comparatively busy waters around Big Sur. These California sea otters are only subtly different, genetically and morphologically, from the northern sea otters. Historically, when otter populations were more or less contiguous throughout the northern Pacific, otters would have occasionally dispersed themselves, and thus their genes, among adjacent populations. This gene flow tends to keep different populations or subspecies from significantly diverging.

Today, reintroduced sea otters are well established on the outer coasts of British Columbia and Washington, and populations in Russia and Alaska are large and considered secure. Oil spills, such as the Exxon Valdez disaster, remain the most serious threat. For instance, an oil spill in British Columbia waters, where offshore drilling and major pipelines are being considered, could threaten much of the provincial population, which is concentrated along the northwestern half of Vancouver Island. However, the fact that there are now more than 100,000 sea otters dispersed among numerous self-sustaining wild populations is one of the great conservation success stories of the twentieth century.

The fate of the California sea otters is less secure. From the original fifty otters, the population has grown continuously since 1911, and it now seems to be leveling off at about three thousand individuals. Again, the primary concern is that an oil spill could wipe out much of the population, which is geograph-ically concentrated in pockets along only a couple hundred miles of coastline.

We make it all the way to Santa Cruz without seeing a sea otter. Then, suddenly, both kids wake up an ugly mix of hungry and angry—hangry. We stop to feed at a local diner. Then we head back to our moist, cold campsite.

Weatherwise, the next day is a repeat of the previous one. The drizzle on the tent provides no incentive to get out from under the duvet. When we do emerge, the sky is a uniform gray. But the condors beckon us nonetheless.

Again, we drive along Highway 1, but the fog is thick the entire stretch. From the lookouts, there is nothing to see—we are in the center of a cloud trying to peer out.

We cut the condor search short and drive to the more prom-ising otter locations we visited yesterday. There are guided boat tours that guarantee otter sightings, but I prefer to find one ourselves, if possible. Our second stop is at Moss Landing State Beach, and right there, much to my surprise, is a sea otter—high fives all around! The otter is lounging on its back, maybe sixty feet from shore. Even without binoculars, I can see that it is eat-ing a crab. We spend an hour watching and photographing the agreeable otter before turning our attention to the other wildlife. From that one location I also photograph great egrets, marbled godwits, whimbrels, brown pelicans, and even a few rare white pelicans. The white pelicans, which were ravaged by DDT, are still a species of concern in parts of their range.

That night, lying in the tent, we decide to move to Big Sur State Park, which was completely full when we first arrived. The new campsite, which is much closer to the prime condor areas, will allow us to increase our condor search time. Having spent three full days looking for this bird with only one possible sighting, it is time to get serious. Briana is even more disappointed than I am that we have yet to really see a condor. She is new to birding and she was, I think, expecting it to be easier to find the largest bird on the continent. I tell her that I once spent a whole summer looking for wolves but only managed to see tracks.

Sea otter

"But we can't spend the whole summer looking for a condor," she says. "We've got to get all the way to Florida."

"True," I say. "Condor time is running out."

The next day, we pack down our camp on Fremont Peak, lunch in Monterey, and then set up our camp at Big Sur, all of which takes most of the day. We spend that evening hiking alongside the ocean, eyes to the sky. The weather has cleared and the vultures are back, but no condors darken the sky. The sunset, however, is spectacular.

I get up in the predawn, 4:45, and head out for a little solo condor searching. It is too early for condors to be soaring, but I hope to find one roosting—the local birders we've met along the highway over the past few days have told us about a few condor hot spots. I don't find any condors, but the morning is lovely and bright. There should be good thermals later in the day.

The family unit heads out again at 10 AM. We are only a few miles south of Big Sur when Briana starts yelling, "Condor! Condor!"

I pull off the highway at the first available pullout. We grab our binoculars and jump out of the van. There are three condors below us, gliding in circles along the cliff face. Another two are

California condor

perched a few hundred yards away on the cliff above the road. One of the condors below us glides right past, but it is hugging the cliff and we only see it in glimpses when it circles away.

I am adjusting my camera's settings for the bright light when Briana yells out again. I look behind me just as a condor crests the cliff and sails over the pullout and right over Briana. It seems as if the condor could have grazed Briana's curly hair had it lowered its talons, but in reality it was probably twenty feet above her. The bird is a huge adult with a bald orange head. The wingspan is enormous, of course, but the body has real mass to it, too. I can even hear the wind pushed by its mighty wings. Although I miss taking the picture, that condor sighting, gliding just above Briana, immediately becomes my favorite bird sighting of all time.

Although none of the other condors come as close as that first one, all five of them end up gliding right past us, both above and below. There are three adults and two juveniles, all of them boldly tagged. Ignoring the screaming kids who are still strapped into their car seats, we finally get some good condor pictures.

Then a California Highway Patrol cruiser pulls over right next to us. I figure the cop is going to tell us that we are illegally parked or something, but he jumps out of the cruiser with too much energy for such a mundane task. He races to the trunk, opens it, and pulls out a shotgun—no, a tripod! He is here for the condors, too. We stand shoulder to shoulder and rattle off shots like we're at a shooting gallery.

"Hell of a bird," he finally says.

"We came all the way from Canada to see one," I say.

"Thanks for visiting California," he says.

That night, we celebrate the condor sightings by drinking a bottle of Yellow Tail shiraz that we bought for $4.99, a price that somewhat dampens my good mood, because the same bottle costs $14.99 in Vancouver. WTF?

California sea otters–check. California condors—check. Satisfied, we say good-bye to the Pacific and turn the van eastward. We are already a week behind our very rough schedule, but we are not too fussed about it. Having finally seen some condors up close and personal, I would describe our moods as jaunty.

Of all the endangered species on our list, the condors are the species I wanted to see the most. Not only are they the species on our list that I suspect has the greatest probability of extinction in the next decades, but they are also unique. If Florida panthers were to go extinct, which could certainly happen, it would not be as great a loss, because they are genetically very similar to other cougar populations. In fact, cougars from Texas populations were recently used to supplement the faltering Florida population. Whooping cranes and Atlantic right whales are also in real trouble, but at least they are reproducing in the wild. And the spotted owl will only go extinct if it is replaced by its close relative the barred owl. But, if the condor disappears, a unique twig on the tree of life is gone, pruned at the base.

Some people, even within conservation circles, believe the dollars that are spent on condor conservation are not wisely spent and could be better put toward more cooperative species. Their position is that the condors have been heading toward extinction for the past ten thousand years. Condors are, they argue, a species designed by natural selection to eat the carcasses of giant ground sloths and mammoths, not road-killed raccoons. Extinction, they argue, is a natural process, one that is being inhibited by intensive management and taxpayer dollars.

There may be some validity to this opinion, but there is also no question that humans helped push condors toward extinction. We did not push condors with the extreme vigor with which we pushed sea otters, but we pushed them nonetheless. Teasing apart the relative roles that nature and humans played in the demise of the condor will be impossible. Therefore, is it not prudent to try to save this species? In a world chock-full of Lamborghinis and fighter jets—and we saw lots of both in supposedly bankrupt California—the dollars spent on condors seem incredibly modest.

In photographs, condors almost always look ungainly; when perched, their large heads seem to bobble back and forth in a slow-witted manner. One could almost be forgiven for thinking that they are Paleolithic relics, a species that is a little long in the tooth. But in flight, they show amazing vitality. The one that almost clipped Briana looked downright muscular, certainly more phoenix than dodo. Seeing them gives me hope that perhaps they will persist over the long term.

But if you really want to see one, I would do so soon.

THREE

desert
LOVE

"I think the American West really
attracts me because it's romantic. The desert,
the empty space, the drama."
ANG LEE, in an interview by Rebecca Murray

The next species on our list is the bristlecone pine tree, which, aside from being endangered, is textbook famous for being the oldest living organism on the planet at around 4,800 years old. Bristlecones live at high elevation in eastern California, where, under harsh conditions, they grow very slowly into oversized bonsai trees. The most direct route from the coast to an accessible grove, according to Google Maps, is to drive through Yosemite National Park on Highway 120 and then up into the White Mountains of the eastern Sierras.

We commit to this route without further research, meandering across California's intensely farmed central valley and then north toward Yosemite. We are almost at the start of

Highway 120 when we bomb past a sign describing the highway conditions through the local mountain passes.

"Did that sign say Highway 120 is closed?"

"I think so."

We go back and stare at the sign, which clearly indicates that not only is Highway 120 closed but also all of the local passes are still closed for the season.

"I thought the highways would be open by mid-May," Briana says.

"I didn't even think about it," I say.

We consult our new California map.

"There's no way through the mountains," Briana says. "We have to go around."

"If we go around to the south," I say, "we can look for a desert tortoise and then try to see a bristlecone on our way back up to Yellowstone."

"It's such a long way around," Briana says.

"We don't really have any other choice," I say.

"No," Briana says, "I guess not."

So we start heading south around the Sierra Nevada mountains.

We spend that night in a roadside motel rather than in glorious Yosemite. Then, in the morning, we stop at REI, where we buy a large rooftop storage box for the van. The box is about the size and shape of a coffin. Perfect, I think, I can ride up top on tough days.

A couple of days later, we are camped in the spectacular Mojave Desert at Red Rock Canyon State Park, a little north of Edwards Air Force Base and the town of Mojave. The desert biome is a stark contrast to Mediterranean California but feels especially foreign in contrast to the lush temperate rain forests of home. We are nineteen days into our trip, and home now feels a long way away, physically and mentally.

We set up our tent right next to an eroded cliff that provides some much-needed shade starting in late afternoon. It is hot, but not brutally hot—maybe a high of ninety degrees Fahrenheit. Given the low humidity, it is bearable even at midday, if you can find a bit of shade. The park ranger tells us that it has been unusually cool all spring.

"You folks picked the right time of year to visit," she says. "This really isn't a summer park—a month from now it'll be 120 degrees every day."

Campsite in the Mojave

Mysterious canyons penetrate the multicolored cliffs, xeric shrubs and plump cacti eke out a modest existence, and bone-dry creek beds crisscross the parched landscape. The light is desert light, harsh and overexposed at midday, subtly colored and textured whenever the sun is near the horizon. The landscape is wide open, almost beckoning, but dangerous, too. Brora and I venture a little way into the scrub, sampling the smells and sounds.

That evening, the sun sets pumpkin orange. Then, the sky slowly ripens to a deep aubergine. Finally, the stars appear, a million of them against the pitch-black sky. An hour later, the moon rises above the cliff, and the moonlight is bright enough to cast strong shadows. Coyotes yap in the distance; a great-horned owl hoots. I have not spent a lot of time in desert habitat, but I always love it.

The next morning, I wake early, when brighter stars still dominate the western sky and direct sunlight is still an hour away. Adie and I walk into the desert, following a dry creek bed up one of the canyons. Although I am only planning on a two-hour stroll, I am careful to take a good look at the landmarks, the mountains and cliffs that surround this basin—getting lost in a desert is deadly serious.

Finn and Brora in the Mojave

I am looking for a desert tortoise, of course, but I'm really just looking. The desert sands have captured the night's activity in a series of tracks, from those of tiny mouse to lone coyote to numerous jackrabbits. The birds, which are keeping their distance, frolic in the scrub—I get good views of a ladder-backed woodpecker and a sage thrasher, one new to me and one not. I wish I were a botanist, however, because it is the plants that really captivate me here, from tiny purple-flowered succulents to large pink-flowered cacti.

Back at the campsite, Briana is making pancakes.

"It's already too hot to sleep in the tent," she says. "We'll need to get out of the sun soon."

I get the kids up and we scarf down pancakes: one for Finny, one for Brora, one for Adie, one for Briana, and about ten for me. Then we get in the van, crank up the AC, and head out to look for a desert tortoise.

Desert tortoises are about the size and shape of a bike helmet and the color of gravel. Typical of the tortoise family,

Testudinidae, desert tortoises have long life spans, up to eighty years, and low mortality rates once they reach adulthood, though they are exceptionally vulnerable to a variety of threats as juveniles. They are adept at digging burrows and spend much of their long lives underground—the best way to avoid the midday sun in the treeless desert. Occasionally, when the temperature is neither too hot nor too cold, they crawl out of their burrows and munch on some vegetation. The burrows of the tortoise are used by so many other species, providing critical refuges from heat and cold, that the desert tortoise is known as an ecosystem engineer, a specific type of keystone species that creates habitat critical to many other species. The classic example of an ecosystem engineer is the beaver, which, by constructing dams across streams, creates beaver ponds—critical habitat for many species.

The primary threats to desert tortoises are habitat loss, the illegal pet trade, accidental roadkills, and predation. In an extreme example of habitat loss, a recent expansion of an army base in the northern Mojave required the relocation of more than seven hundred tortoises, but the project was halted midstream after many of the relocated tortoises died—relocation is always a tricky business. The pet trade is a threat to numerous endangered reptiles, which are often slow enough to be easily caught and cool enough to be in great demand. In prime tortoise habitat, roadkills have been reduced by erecting roadside fences, but the fences are expensive to build and maintain, and they also carve up once-contiguous populations into isolated fragments. Humans can cause the number of predators to increase by, for example, providing food sources such as garbage. For this reason, ravens, which eat young tortoise hatchlings, are now more numerous near desert towns.

Although there are still many thousands of desert tortoises left in the wild, life is tough for them.

Recently, on the basis of genetic and behavioral differences, the desert tortoise has been split into two species, the Mojave desert tortoise (*Gopherus agassizii*) and the Sonoran desert tortoise (*Gopherus morafkai*). Such species splitting is a common occurrence, especially now that DNA sequence data can highlight differences that are difficult to recognize, even with careful observation and measurement. But what happened historically to cause these genetic differences to accumulate and to produce two species from one? This is the question that haunted Charles Darwin and that he so thoroughly answered with the publication of *On the Origin of Species* in 1859.

Typically, a geological barrier splits the original population into two or more isolated populations. If the barrier is solid and permanent, the populations start to diverge as natural selection adapts the tortoises to their respective environments; additionally, random genetic mutations that occur in one population are not shared with the other. Over many millennia, the once-identical populations become genetically more and more distinct. Eventually, the differences become big enough to justify classifying the separate populations as separate species. In the case of the desert tortoise, the geological barrier between Mojave and Sonoran populations was the Colorado River, and the split occurred perhaps a million years ago. Basically, some turtles managed to cross the river, resulting in two isolated populations. A million years later, there are two species where once there was one.

So there we are, driving through the Mojave Desert, looking not for a desert tortoise but rather a Mojave desert tortoise. If we don't find one around here, our plan is to drive into Arizona and look for a Sonoran desert tortoise, since this species is more numerous. We start our search right in the campground by walking the trails where the park warden mentioned she has seen tortoises in the past.

"The trick is to look at the right time of the day," the warden says. "Too early or too late and they'll be in their burrows."

Unsuccessful on the campground trails, we drive slowly along a series of gravel roads looking for an oddly shaped rock in a landscape full of oddly shaped rocks. The hopefully named Desert Tortoise Natural Area is north of California City, and we try zigzag-

Looking for desert tortoises in the Mojave

ging in that general direction on a series of increasingly dodgy back roads—gravel, dirt, two-track, and finally an ATV trail. My great concern is that we will get stuck in the backcountry. With this outcome in mind, I previously filled every vessel we have, five gallons' worth in total, with drinking water, the limiting resource in this environment—the resource in shortest supply relative to its demand.

The ATV trail dead-ends into a dry salt lake. We get out of the van and walk across the white salt flats, which reflect the brilliant sunshine. Even through sunglasses and squinted eyes, the entire landscape looks overexposed by three stops. Rusty car parts and a long-abandoned railway line suggest that humans have been here at some point, but we can see a long way in every direction and are utterly alone. There is an otherworldly feel to the landscape, more Tatooine or Arrakis than our blue planet.

We backtrack along the ATV trail. Then we cut south on a two-track in hopes of circling the salt lake. In the middle of nowhere, we find a sign that says "Caution Desert Tortoise." We take this to be a good omen. The sign is sun faded and barely legible because it has been blasted with a shotgun. We take this to be a bad omen. We park at the sign and walk across the scrubby plain, poking each rock in hopes that a head might pop out. The sun glares down relentlessly.

Desert tortoise

Back in the van, we creep along at two miles per hour. We are only a few hundred yards past the sign when I see a rock that looks suspicious. I study the rock through my binoculars—desert tortoise!

Leaving Adie in the van, we get out and walk slowly toward the tortoise, which is sitting motionless in the shade of a scrubby sagebrush. We stop about thirty feet from the tortoise and take the required one hundred photographs, all of which are almost identically bad. I tiptoe a little closer for a portrait shot with the telephoto lens. The subject really is a handsome specimen—the shell is quite bulbous, each protective scute is lined with a series of growth rings like the cross-section of an old tree, and its leathery head and limbs protrude just enough to convince us that it is of biological and not geological origins. I back away from the tortoise and survey the landscape—sun-baked plain, dry salt lake, three abandoned railcars, and brown mountains in the far distance.

"How can anything survive out here?" Briana asks, before rushing the kids back to the van for liquids.

I sit cross-legged in the sand and study the tortoise for perhaps half an hour—it barely moves—and I come no closer to answering Briana's question.

After we have seen the tortoise and, eventually, consumed a roadside lunch, the kids fall fast asleep in their car seats. We drive a leisurely loop through the northwestern Mojave, which is the easiest way to avoid the midday sun. The quiet drive also gives me the opportunity to ask Briana about a possible itinerary change.

"I was thinking that we should skip going to southern Arizona to look for a jaguar," I say. The jaguar was the next species on our list.

"Why?" Briana asks.

My long-winded rationale is threefold: (1) we're already way behind schedule; (2) it seems too far to go for a species that we won't see, especially considering that going all the way there and then all the way back to see a bristlecone pine would mean a 1,200-mile round-trip; and (3) we were going all the way there to spend a day or two in jaguar habitat, not to see an actual jaguar, but since jaguars used to range throughout the Mojave, too, we can simply use the Mojave as our historical jaguar habitat.

"They used to live here?" Briana interjects. "I think of jaguars as living in jungles."

"They prefer jungle, I think, but they can live in a lot of different habitats, even scrubby desert. Historically, they ranged throughout the southwest at low densities—all the way to Los Angeles. There are still populations ranging from northern Mexico through to northern Argentina. But the large range is deceptive, because they are in trouble in almost every jurisdiction."

"And there definitely aren't any jaguars left in the U.S.?" she asks.

"The last jaguar was wandering around southern Arizona for a few years before the government decided to tranquilize it and put a radio collar on it in 2009. It was dead a few weeks later—supposedly of kidney failure, but that probably had something to do with the collaring and tranquilizers. As far as anyone knows, that individual was the very last jaguar north of the Mexican border. Now, with the border fence and all the patrolling rednecks, it seems unlikely that any more will wander north from Mexico." (While editing a first draft of this book in December 2011, there was, to my surprise, a confirmed sighting of a jaguar in southern Arizona.)

"Damn minutemen," she says.

And so, instead of forging on to southern Arizona, we will head back north to see a bristlecone pine and then cut east toward Yellowstone—a route change that relieves both of us. We will be back on schedule, more or less, which means we get to spend an extra day or two relaxing in the Mojave. More time playing and less time driving already seems like a great idea.

How in the hell, I wonder to myself, will we ever make it all the way to Florida?

FOUR

among
THE ANCIENTS

"What you've done becomes the judge
of what you're going to do—especially in other
people's minds. When you're traveling,
you are what you are right there and then.
People don't have your past to hold against you.
No yesterdays on the road."

WILLIAM LEAST HEAT-MOON, *Blue Highways*

A couple of days later, we drive north out of the Mojave on Highway 395, which is bordered by the Sierra Nevada mountains to the west and the White Mountains to the east. Mount Whitney, the highest peak in the contiguous United States at 14,505 feet, is among the many scenic peaks.

We are heading for the Ancient Bristlecone Pine Forest, which is nestled high above the valley at the top of the White Mountains. First, though, we stop at a well-manned tourist information center to verify our directions. The nice lady behind the counter has actually been up to the ancient forest herself in previous years.

"That forest is a heck of a long ways up," she says.

Then she asks rhetorically—"Is that road even open yet? Let me hop on the radio and check." In less than two minutes, she determines that the road opened three days ago. "It sounds like you can drive right up to the visitor's center," she says, "except that some arsonist burned it to the ground two years ago."

Directions confirmed, we drive north to the town of Big Pine. There we get off the main highway and start climbing up into the White Mountains. The elevation of the valley floor is about four thousand feet, and the bristlecone forest starts around ten thousand feet, so it really is a long climb. The minivan, which has performed heroically thus far, huffs and puffs up the incessant switchbacks.

Around nine thousand feet, we stop at a scenic lookout. The Sierra Nevada range across the valley catches most of the precipitation and is still buried deep in snow. The valley is obviously in a strong rain shadow, because it already looks like a dust bowl despite the moist spring. We have a snack, pop our ears, and watch a mountain bluebird hop from branch to branch on a dead tree—it looks like a Christmas ornament in an otherwise stark landscape. Then, just as we are getting ready to continue upward, a couple ride up on their bikes. Briana is jealous.

"Wow," she says. "Did you ride all the way up?"

"Yeah," they say too casually.

"We were having trouble driving up," Briana says truthfully.

Above nine thousand feet, the road is flanked by patchy snow, but we make it to the parking lot at 9,800 feet nonetheless. There I load Finn into our baby carrier, which I've taken to calling the Man Uterus, and grab Adie's leash. Then we start hiking up and into the ancient forest at Brora's pace—start with some mad running and then stop and look under every rock. I try to convince Brora that it is the trees that are particularly fascinating here, but she is in a rock phase today.

In contrast to our condor search, we have no difficulty finding a bristlecone pine tree (*Pinus longaeva*)—almost every tree in this forest is a bristlecone. I walk up to the first large tree, which is a gnarly thirty feet tall, and feel the rough bark. I stroke the short needles that are bundled in bushy packets of five. Then I find a cone on the ground, which really is bristly from protruding little spines. I shake the cone and watch the last couple of seeds that it contains flutter to the ground. With a moistened fingertip, I pick up one of the seeds and show it to Brora and Finn.

"In a couple of thousand years," I say, "this seed might turn into a big tree."

Time is still meaningless to them, of course, but I think it is neat to be among such old organisms in the presence of ones that are so young.

The forest we hike into is called the Schulman Grove, named for Dr. Edmund Schulman, the scientist who first determined the incredible longevity of bristlecone trees in the area in 1957. Schulman was a pioneer in the rather exclusive field of dendroclimatology. Dendroclimatologists correlate historical tree growth to historical climatic conditions and use this information to estimate climatic parameters such as drought frequency. Schulman would have started this process by first ageing a tree, a feat accomplished by taking a core sample and then counting growth rings. Schulman had aged conifer trees throughout the West, some of which were more than a thousand years old, but he was unprepared for the incredible longevity of the bristlecones. One tree he studied, now named Methuselah after the long-lived biblical character, was estimated to have a germination date of 2832 BCE—a couple hundred years before construction began on the first pyramids. At 4,844 years, Methuselah is still believed to be the oldest living organism in the world, and it is still in this forest somewhere, though the tree is unmarked to prevent vandalism. This lack of disclosure is undoubtedly a good idea given the recent arson—Methuselah is definitely not a tree you want a bunch of yahoos carving their initials into.

Adie and me with bristlecone pine

We continue hiking up into the forest. The surrounding landscape is a harsh mix of bare scree slopes and patchy snow—at this altitude the spartan grove of bristlecones constitutes a lush Eden of sorts, albeit one older than the fictional Eden itself. The trail gains a little elevation—perhaps a few hundred feet—and I find myself breathing deeply to fill my lungs. At ten thousand feet, a volume of air contains about 30 percent fewer oxygen molecules than it did at sea level, and without any time to acclimate, the difference is painfully noticeable. With a sleeping Finn strapped to my belly like a cannonball, I plod along the trail like a leaden-footed Frankenstein, stopping every few minutes to catch my breath among the bristlecones.

We spend a couple of hours slowly exploring the forest. I insist Briana and Brora smell, feel, taste, and, of course, hug the various parts of the bristlecones. As we near the parking lot, it starts to snow, icy little flakes that are driven by a suddenly harsh wind. Then, just as we start driving down the mountain, a bona fide blizzard erupts. The switchbacks, which were harrowing on the way up, are now downright treacherous. Visibility drops to about ten feet.

"Shit," I say to myself. "Do we stop and get stuck here for the night, or do we keep going and slide into a ditch?"

Three minutes later, the blizzard abates and the sky breaks into patchy blue. The vagaries of altitude.

That night, we stay at a motel in Bishop, California, a town near the Nevada border that is famous for pack mules and rock climbing. We eat dinner at a busy Mexican restaurant and then stroll along the main strip. We retire to our room early. Brora watches the dreaded TV (*Max and Ruby*), Briana sends a bunch of emails, and I convalesce in bed with Finn—it is now painfully obvious that I have a full-blown case of poison oak.

Poison oak was growing everywhere along the coast. We saw poison oak in every campground, especially on Fremont Peak, where it seemed to comprise most of the undergrowth. There my primary parenting responsibility was to keep Brora out of the shrubbery. But, thinking back, I didn't necessarily take proper precautions myself. At least twice, I walked bare legged and barefoot into thick undergrowth—once to get a better angle for a photo of a western bluebird and once to return a wild turkey chick to its cheeping brood after Adie carried it back to our campsite. Another possibility is that Adie brought the toxic oils back to our campsite on her fur after tearing her way through the underbrush. Since she sleeps at my feet every night, she may well have transferred the oils to my unsuspecting legs.

I have had poison ivy a few times, but each time it was a mild rash easily cured with a little hydrocortisone cream. Poison oak is a whole different beast. It started as we left Big Sur, with an itchy rash on my legs below my knees. I applied a little hydrocortisone and forgot about it for a couple of days. Then a bunch of clear blisters formed on top of the increasingly itchy rash. By the time we reached the Mojave, these blisters were rupturing and leaving a series of large open sores, each seeping a disgusting yellow fluid. Now, in Bishop, the seeping continues unabated, my ankles are swollen to almost twice their normal size, and the rash now looks like second degree burns. Even walking has become difficult. And to make matters worse, my mood parallels my worsening symptoms.

A pharmacist in Bishop confirms what I have already read on the Internet—there is really nothing to do except apply hydrocortisone cream and wait a few weeks for the outbreak to run its course. Apparently only particularly nasty cases require hospitalization and the injection of corticosteroids.

"It's a real pain for the Forest Service," he says. "It causes more sick days than the flu."

That night, I do not sleep at all. Instead, I lie there and scratch at my seeping, burning legs. Around two in the morning, I get out of bed, pull on some clothes, and go for a hobble around the deserted town. I force Adie to go with me just so that I have someone to bitch at.

The police car pulls up next to me as I reach the end of the main strip. The two officers in the car are primarily interested in Adie.

"What kind of dog is that?"

"Blue heeler."

The older officer in the passenger seat turns toward the driver, who looks like he is still in high school. "Told you so," he says. Then he looks back at me. "Real smart dogs," he says.

"Every one except this one," I say.

"And what," he asks, "are you up to?"

So we talk for fifteen minutes about poison oak and Canada and family road trips. It is a leisurely conversation, not an inquisition—they are obviously bored on a quiet night in a quiet town.

Back in the motel room, I toss and turn until Briana gets up at seven o'clock and has a shower. I hobble down to the breakfast room for a cup of yellowish coffee, which is almost the same color as the secretions dripping down my legs and certainly no color coffee should ever be.

FIVE

the loneliest
ROAD

"As we crossed the Colorado-Utah border
I saw God in the sky in the form of
huge sunburning clouds above the desert that
seemed to point a finger at me and say,
'Pass here and go on, you're on the road to heaven.'"
JACK KEROUAC, *On the Road*

Driving across central Nevada is a bit like driving across the moon. The road we pick, Route 6, is only serviced by two crappy towns, Tonopah and Ely, for its entire three-hundred-mile stretch through Nevada. With good reason, Route 6 is described as one of the loneliest roads in America. Driving at sixty-five miles per hour, we only encounter another car going the opposite direction about every fifteen minutes, which is pretty damn empty for a primary highway.

Route 6 cuts a beeline across the Great Basin ecoregion, a vast area that doesn't drain any water to the oceans via rivers—any rain that falls in a basin is retained there, except for groundwater seepage and evaporation. The Great Basin is actually composed of many smaller basins separated by minor mountain ranges, and as we peak each mountain range, we can see the next basin, the empty road, and the next mountain range. We can see where we will be driving in twenty minutes.

Driving across Nevada

I am enchanted by the empty, open landscape. Perhaps living in a temperate rain forest for the past fifteen years has left me craving open spaces. I like the big skies, the desperate vegetation, the deeply ribbed burros, the scrappy magpies, and always being able to see the horizon. This is an inhospitable landscape, suited to scorpions and bombing ranges, and yet I find myself wondering about real estate prices. How much Nevada ranch could we get in exchange for our Vancouver bungalow? Fanciful dreaming like this sustains me when the van is quiet and the road seemingly endless.

At last, as we drive into the depths of the Great Basin, our road trip starts feeling a little Kerouac-like. We have been away from home long enough now that that life is fading, and there is still a lot of trip left, so we have not yet started to imagine our return to it. Right now, as Kerouac said, life is the road.

Of course, if you, like Kerouac, want to spend a portion of your life on the road, you will need a vehicle. When we first started to look for a suitable vehicle for the road trip, we wanted to buy a used RV that was large enough to sleep all of us comfortably but small enough to drive through a city without too much fuss. But buying a used RV turned into a nightmare of funky smells and nasty stains. Our initial plan was to spend $10,000 on an RV, drive the crap out of it for six months, making some stains of our own along the way, and then unload it for $9,000 on some eager tourists looking to experience the back roads of Canada.

But it quickly became apparent that $10,000 wasn't enough. Briana vetoed every moldy caravan under that price within the Greater Vancouver area; one RV showed promise but had no engine, another had an engine but also seemed to house chickens, and even I had no interest in driving across the country in a chicken coop. So we upped our spending limit and reduced our expectations.

Finally, after much Craigslist-ing and a lot of haggling with local dealers, we walked away in a huff from the moldy RVs and overpriced Euro-trash-vans and settled instead on a "mint" 2008 Dodge Grand Caravan with 46,000 miles on the odometer. It didn't have all the room we wanted, but it drove well and promised not to be a major money pit—plus the price, $13,000, was about right.

Importantly, the gas mileage was also much better than the typical RV's, which made us feel a little better about our carbon emissions. To reduce our carbon emissions on the trip, we had contemplated buying a hybrid vehicle or purchasing carbon offsets, but such attempts at greening the trip seemed like little more than window dressing. Hybrid vehicles, in addition to being beyond our budget and requiring a lot of rare earth metals to build, are not particularly efficient on the highway, where brakes are not applied often enough to recharge batteries—plus the fact that you can buy a hybrid Cadillac Escalade for $85,000 makes me suspicious of the whole hybrid genre. Carbon offsets, which would involve paying someone to somehow store enough carbon to offset our excessive burning of fossil fuels, also make me nervous, because they seem like an overly easy way for the wealthy to justify more consumption and they also seem particularly prone to eco-fraud (as in you pay someone to sequester carbon but they don't). So we are momentarily emitting like the rich and famous (e.g., Al Gore) and trying not to feel too bad about it. And although our road trip obviously has a big carbon footprint, a family trip to Europe, as was Briana's wish, would have had a much larger carbon footprint because air travel is such a huge contributor to climate change.

Did we make the right vehicle choice? It would certainly be nice to have an RV on occasion, but a decent RV would have cost perhaps $30,000, and the difference in cost between an RV and the Caravan is more than sufficient to fund the rest of our trip—motels, food, gas, etc. So, after twenty-three days on the road, our trusty Caravan does feel like the right vehicle given our budget constraints—enough vehicle, but not too much. Even the harshest stretches of the loneliest road in America haven't fazed our lovely Caravan.

Ely, Nevada, is a rough town, more waypoint than municipality, a place to kick the tires and quickly refuel. But if we do not stay here for the night, it will be a long way to anywhere else. Besides, today is my birthday and I don't want to spend the whole day driving.

We get the last room at a family-run motel. The people are friendly, but the room is in need of some updating, right down to the shag carpet. Why is it that every motel room in North America is still carpeted? Would not some hardwood flooring or even some linoleum make travelers a little happier? Walking across this shag carpet in bare feet reveals a marvel of textures—every spill or, God forbid, excretion since 1975 has left its crusty scar on this carpet.

The heavily pregnant eighteen-year-old girl working reception at the motel recommends the Mexican restaurant down the street, which is the only busy spot in this four-restaurant town. The food is okay, I guess, but almost indistinguishable from the Mexican food we had in Bishop a couple of nights ago. This time, instead of burritos, I have enchiladas, but as far as I can tell it is all the same slop served a slightly different way.

Back at the motel, Briana plays with the kids outside while I ice my poison oak, which is nastier than ever. Then I get to work on my birthday present from Briana—a six-pack and the remote control. It is the best birthday present ever.

A couple of days later, we are camped maybe ten miles north of Vernal, Utah, in the northeastern corner of the state. We are heading toward Yellowstone National Park, but we have detoured to this location to look for a sage grouse. Like the desert tortoise, the sage grouse was recently split into two species, the greater sage grouse (*Centrocercus urophasianus*) and the Gunnison sage grouse (*Centrocercus minimus*). So, in this location, I guess we are actually looking for a greater sage grouse.

Although we have been traveling fast for us, we were still able to notice that Utah contains a particularly beautiful mix of salt flats and lofty mountains, flat-topped buttes and red rock canyons. No wonder Brigham Young was able to convince the Mormons to stop here—I would have stopped, too. So far, the Mormons, God love 'em, have presented no obstacles to our passage, though I have taken the precaution of slapping a little duct tape over the Darwin fish bumper sticker. Our biggest complaint is that there do not seem to be any coffee shops anywhere—caffeine, along with most other pleasures, is apparently a no-no for the Latter Day Saints.

The campground is empty except for a group of paleontologists from the University of Miami, who tell us that the surrounding hillsides contain a treasure trove of dinosaur fossils. We are happy for the company and figure that if the Mormons get restless, they'll lynch the damn paleontologists first. Before climbing into the tent for the night, we exhaust ourselves running madly around the campground, and Adie exhausts herself madly chasing ground squirrels from burrow to burrow.

I wake before my alarm, at 3:45 AM, and we—Adie and I— are on the road in minutes. I am heading for nearby Diamond Mountain, where the surrounding flats supposedly harbor a decent number of greater sage grouse. My first problem, however, is that "Diamond Mountain" is a colloquial name used for at least three nearby hills, presumably any mound that ever coughed up a diamond from one of the many local mines. The best info I have, from some Utah birders, points me toward the Diamond Mountain that lies ten miles northeast of Vernal, so that is where I head.

Sage grouse are the largest grouse in North America. Despite their scarcity, they still range across much of the western United States and nip into Canada in the southern Prairies. There was even a small population in British Columbia a century ago, but that population succumbed to the impacts of livestock grazing, agriculture, and hunting—the same pressures that threaten sage grouse everywhere. The population in

Utah is still large enough to allow a carefully regulated hunt in certain counties, this one included.

Sage grouse are most famous for their elaborate courtship rituals, in which the males gather together in breeding aggregations called leks. The males strut around in the leks and billow their vocal sacs, which when inflated look like a rather impressive set of mammary glands. Via all the strutting and cleavage wagging, the males try to convince as many females as possible to mate with them. Typically, one or two males will dominate the lek, and most of the females will mate with them. The females then disappear into the sagebrush to raise their brood entirely alone. Unfortunately for me, it is probably too late in the season to witness a lek in action.

By first light, I am on the slopes of Diamond Mountain, a modest hill compared with the mountains we've seen on this trip. The habitat looks good (at least there is a lot of sagebrush, the primary habitat requirement for sage grouse). I drive the gravel roads that crisscross the mountain's flanks at ten miles per hour. Right away, while it is still mainly dark, the headlights illuminate a potential candidate.

That was easy, I think, reaching for my binoculars. But the binoculars reveal a female ring-necked pheasant, an introduced exotic that is well established across much of North America.

In time to see/feel the sunrise, I get out of the van and walk across the sagebrush-covered slopes. I contemplate leaving Adie in the van, but she is itching to run, and perhaps her exuberance will flush a hidden grouse. (Normally, I would not encourage such behavior, but this is not a protected area; rather, it is ranchland, with lots of dogs, cattle, and ATVs). I walk to the top of a ridge and survey the rolling landscape that is carpeted in patches of olive-colored sagebrush. Then I walk the long way back to the van, zigzagging between patches of sagebrush but flushing only sparrows.

I spend the next five hours driving down farm roads at ten miles per hour and running madly through the sagebrush, but the sage grouse continue to evade me.

"I should have gotten more specific directions," I grumble to myself. "I should have asked a local birder to take me out."

After our earlier successes, I was clearly overconfident in my ability to find a sage grouse this morning. Finally, I head back to the campsite. My only solace is that I will have several more chances to see sage grouse at other stops along our route—I'm momentarily foiled but not without hope.

I get back to the campsite at noon, an hour later than my latest estimated time of arrival. Briana already has the campsite packed down. I load the van lickety-split. Then we drive north toward Wyoming.

The drive into Wyoming on Route 191 is spectacular. The road is utterly empty, the landscape is high-altitude desert and sagebrush steppe, and the weather is wild—dark clouds galloping across the big sky, harsh winds blowing the van sideways on the plateaus, and icy flurries gusting whenever the route tops eight thousand feet. Twice, we take dirt side roads into the sagebrush, ostensibly to look for sage grouse but really just to look.

After the beautiful drive, we spend the night in Rock Springs, which is the most miserable town of the trip so far. The weather, with snow in the air and temperatures below freezing, feels more like March than late May. The surrounding landscape is bleak—bare rock, sooty snow, and a decade's worth of garbage strewn about. And, worst of all, the motels are clearly colluding on price. Every dump is a hundred bucks, plus or minus a dollar.

We buy a few supplies at the huge Walmart, a shopping experience that sucks the life out of us and undoubtedly of the whole town. Then we eat dinner at Subway. Briana wrinkles her nose with every bite into her veggie sub before finally asking me, "Is it just me, or does Subway bread always smell funny?"

The drive from Rock Springs to Yellowstone is complicated by snow. We manage to creep into Jackson, Wyoming, a tourist town near the south entrance of Yellowstone, only because we are able to drive in a plow's wake for the last twenty miles. We were planning on making it all the way to our campsite in the park, but those plans clearly need some tweaking.

"We'll have to stay here," I say.

"If there are any rooms," Briana says. It is, after all, Memorial Day weekend.

"We can't camp in this shit," I say.

"No, we can't," Briana agrees, looking back at little, fragile, smiling Finn.

We have no problem getting a room in Jackson. Because of the weather, there have been a ton of last-minute cancellations. I ask our host at the motel if this weather is normal for Memorial Day weekend. "Snowiest Memorial Day in at least a decade," he tells me. "But we have had snow on July Fourth, so anything is possible in Jackson."

A little Internet access helps illuminate our options. The south and east roads into the park are closed, but they are trying hard to open them. Most of the park is buried in snow, but the northern fringe, which is at a lower altitude, is relatively open. Then, thanks to more last-minute cancellations, we are able to convert our campground reservation into a cabin reservation at the Mammoth Hot Springs Hotel, in the northwest corner of the park. Quaint cabin rather than camping in the snow = good. We spend two days in Jackson waiting for the road to open. Jackson is a typical resort town like Banff or Aspen, not a real town like Ely or Rock Springs, but we appreciate the good coffee and decent Thai food. After ten days of grocery shopping at gas stations and Walmarts, Briana is literally glowing during her visit to the local organic grocery store.

"I love this store," she says, abandoning the kids and dashing toward the produce aisles.

SIX

restless nights
IN GRIZZLY COUNTRY

"If people persist in trespassing
upon the grizzlies' territory, we must accept the fact
that the grizzlies, from time to time,
will harvest a few trespassers."
EDWARD ABBEY, *A Voice Crying in the Wilderness:*
Notes from a Secret Journal

We drive into Yellowstone on Memorial Day. The road is open, but we are warned at the park gate that the road could close at any moment if conditions deteriorate. As the road climbs into the park, the snow deepens, and soon the route is more tunnel than road with ten-foot cliffs of plowed snow lining it. We stop to look at Yellowstone Lake, but it is still frozen solid, more glacier than lake. Then, with flurries dancing, we press on.

Yellowstone National Park is famous for many things. For instance, it was the first national park in the world, it has hundreds of geothermal features, and it has great wildlife-viewing opportunities. The park is also infamous for overcrowding, particularly during July and August, and consequently we planned our visit for May. Local biologists also suggested that May was a much better month for wildlife viewing, but not a single one suggested we would need to bring our snowshoes.

Thankfully, winter turns to spring as we near Mammoth Hot Springs. The elevation of Yellowstone Lake is 7,736 feet, whereas the elevation of Mammoth Hot Springs Hotel is 6,235 feet, and that 1,500-foot difference makes all the difference in the world. The clouds part, revealing a strong summer sun, the temperature goes from twenty-five degrees to forty-five degrees Fahrenheit, and the snow

Briana and Finn in Yellowstone

shrinks to dirty patches. There is even some lawn visible in front of the hotel and a herd of elk methodically mowing it.

Our cabin is perfect: one room, two beds, a shared bathroom out back, and an elk lying in the driveway. Plus, the cabins are pet friendly, and we are allowed to cook on the porch. It's a steal of a deal at $80 a night, given that we are right in the park, especially compared with our crappy $100 motel room in Rock Springs.

Before we can even unload the van, a rumor rustles from cabin to cabin—there is a bear behind the hotel. We walk over and join the gaggle of people watching the little black bear sleeping in a tree.

"Daddy, I'm scared," says Brora as she jumps into my arms.

In my twenties, I spent a field season working as a biologist in Denali National Park in Alaska. The fieldwork was tedious, but the landscape was spectacular. By the end of that summer, my field crew had spent a hundred nights camped out in the Denali backcountry near our study plots.

Every week, we would see grizzlies, usually from a distance across the open alpine tundra. But there were also close encounters. A big male ran right through our campsite while three of us were eating dinner, and another grizzly of undetermined size almost collided with me in a willow thicket. By the end of the field season, one thing was clear—grizzlies gave me nightmares.

In my recurring nightmare, I wake to a commotion in the campsite. I unzip the tent and stick my head out for a look around. What I see in the soft midnight sun is gruesome—a huge grizzly has dragged my coworker out of his tent and is mauling him to death right in front of my tent. I tuck my head back into my tent and look desperately for a weapon, but all I see is my fragile naked body. Then I pull my sleeping bag over my head and cower like a child hiding from a monster under the bed. Soon after this, I jolt awake.

The dream leaves me horrified, not so much by the grizzly attack but rather by my utter lack of courage. I console myself with the knowledge that it was only a dream—I would behave differently if the attack were real. But I also know that if the attack were real, a little courage probably would not make any difference to the outcome of the encounter. When a grizzly attacks, there is not a lot one can do except pull up the blankets and play dead, a dispiriting strategy if ever there was one. If the attacker were a black bear or cougar, some courage would be of use because there is at least some hope that you would prevail in driving away the attacker. But you don't win a fight with a grizzly.

Grizzlies are big, weighing from 400 to 1,500 pounds, though bears in the upper range are typically only found in coastal areas, where they get to gorge seasonally on salmon. Grizzlies (*Ursus arctos horribilis*) are actually a subspecies of the brown bear (*Ursus arctos*), which range throughout the Northern Hemisphere; the term "grizzly" is most applicable to the brown bears of the interior of North America. To differentiate a grizzly from a black bear, look for a large shoulder hump and a flat, almost concave, face. Coat color can be useful, but it can also be misleading—black bears can be tawny and grizzlies can be blackish. Although smaller in size, interior grizzlies are less docile than the huge coastal grizzlies, which often seem mild-mannered in comparison, probably because of all that salmon. Grizzlies are classic omnivores, eating vegetation, berries, seeds, grubs, and, of course, meat whenever the opportunity arises.

Thankfully, attacks by grizzlies are rare. The odds of getting struck by lightning are higher. The odds of getting killed in a traffic accident en route to the park are much higher. Anyone who spends a lot of time working in bear country, particularly grizzly country, is well aware of these favorable statistics, but the bears loom large in the psyche nonetheless. Even wildlife biologists versed in statistical analysis cannot help but be a little preoccupied by the fact that you are always a potential prey item in grizzly country. One biologist I met in Alaska would not take a crap in the woods without bringing a shotgun along with him.

If you are unlucky enough to be attacked by a grizzly, the best strategy is to play dead, though that by no means ensures a positive outcome. Grizzly bears will aggressively defend their territory and food caches, and the idea is to play dead in hopes that the bear will eventually, after a few swipes and nibbles, realize that you are not a territorial threat. The strategy changes if you are attacked by a black bear. A black bear is typically hunting and intends to eat you, so playing dead will only facilitate this outcome. If you are attacked by a black bear, the best strategy (which, again, does not ensure a positive outcome) is to fight back with everything you have. *Bear Attacks* by Stephen Herrero makes for a fascinating read on the subject, though gruesome details left me traumatized when I first read it twenty years ago. Herrero analyzes a century's worth of bear attacks and suggests the above strategies to survive an encounter, though given the low probability of an attack, I wonder if it is not better to simply hike naively and enjoy yourself.

I review Herrero's rules with Briana when we are lying in bed on our first night in Yellowstone, but she just looks at me as if I have lost my mind.

"I'm a feminist," I say. "I expect you to be in the fight with me."

"If everything goes all Stone Age," she says, "you'd better be a frigging caveman."

"Typical," I say. "It's all about equal rights until the check comes or a bear attacks."

The next morning before dawn, I head out on my own for a couple of hours of prebreakfast wildlife viewing. My route options are limited because a rock slide has closed the road across the north side of the park at the eight-mile mark and the park to the south is snowbound. I decide to start by driving the first eight miles of the north road, but it is hard to even get going because there are so many frigging elk everywhere. I take pictures of elk in front of our cabin, in front of the hotel, on the road, on the steps of the post office. It is calving season and I presume that the elk are pressed in close to the town in an attempt to evade the wolves.

Just beyond the town of Mammoth, the north road opens up into a spectacular valley that is littered with large herbivores. Elk, of course, but also hundreds of bison, a smattering of pronghorn and mule deer, and even one lonely moose. I am overwhelmed by the sheer abundance. It is as if I have been transported back in time fifteen thousand years, and I am the first person to cross the Bering land bridge and see North America in all of its prehuman glory, though the diversity would have been even greater back then. I take three hundred pictures, trying without success to capture the feeling of the Neolithic panorama.

Plains bison in Yellowstone

I get out of the van and walk into the valley on one of the hiking trails. In the vehicle I was seemingly invisible, but on foot I am not to be trusted—ears perk and noses twitch, and then the elk and bison part to allow my passage. I hike to the top of a knoll, sit with my back to a large boulder, and watch the sun move into the valley. I slowly scan the valley with the spotting scope, hoping for a grizzly or wolf, but I am more than satisfied with all of the herbivores. Many of the bison have calved within the last few days, and I watch the little cinnamon-colored tykes frolic with each other and then return to their mothers to nurse.

From this perch, it is hard to believe that the plains bison (AKA buffalo) were once almost extinct. At the time of European contact, millions and millions of burly bison roamed North America, and, as a species, they would have constituted one of the largest protein sources on the planet. The geographic range was equally huge, from the Yukon to Mexico and from California to the Atlantic. Despite the vastness of both their numbers and their range, only a few hundred individuals were left by the 1880s. The sole cause of the incredible decline of the plains bison was commercial hunting, a hunt that was typically only for the skins.

Today, although there are hundreds of thousands of bison in North America, most live on farms and are not wild buffalo but rather "beefalo" in the making. Only fifteen thousand individuals or so persist in a relatively wild state, unfenced and free roaming; consequently, they are still considered a species at risk across their range.

Very young plains bison in Yellowstone

All the meat in this valley makes me wonder if this is the natural state of abundance for North America. Should every landscape be similarly chock-full of animals? Or is this unnaturally overcrowded—a result of habitat protection and not enough predation? I had read that elk numbers had been halved since wolves were reintroduced in 1996, but it is hard to imagine more elk than this. Or maybe this ecosystem should actually be more crowded and more diverse, and the only reason it seems so fecund is because I have no truly natural baseline with which to compare it. Daniel Pauly, a fisheries biologist, first outlined the problem of shifting baselines in fisheries management. Fish populations are often managed relative to some baseline population, but the baseline has frequently been determined well after human exploitation began and thus is said to have shifted. Here, sitting next to my boulder, the park road is half a mile away, but I can still hear the traffic and a glance over my shoulder reveals a steady stream of vehicles bisecting the bison herd—far from a natural baseline but still quite spectacular.

I return to our cabin in time to wake everybody and make pancakes on the porch. It is a battle to get Brora to eat anything, but pancakes are a hit right now. While we eat, we watch the three female elk that have taken up residence on the slope behind our cabin. A raven circles overhead; a magpie steals the pancake Finn tosses to the ground. After breakfast, I give the dishes a quick scrape, and then we hit the road in search of grizzlies and wolves.

At the start of my biology career, I spent six field seasons working in Algonquin Provincial Park in central Ontario, which in most years has a resident wolf population of about 250 individuals. Despite this relatively large population, I only saw wolves on perhaps ten separate occasions, though I heard them howling at night more often. Typically, the Algonquin sightings were lightning-fast glimpses, but on three occasions I was lucky enough to spend significant time in their company.

Then, in Alaska, I saw wolves guarding a moose they would eventually kill. This was a weeklong saga in which a rotating series of wolves prevented the young male moose from eating or sleeping, and then, when the moose was sufficiently weakened, the whole pack showed up and killed it without much effort. Unfortunately, or perhaps fortunately, because I had started to feel pretty sorry for the poor moose, I missed the actual kill. By the time I returned from a field site, which was only a few hours after the kill, according to a biologist who witnessed it, a grizzly had usurped the carcass and was already lying on top of it sound asleep.

More recently, in British Columbia, I have seen wolves twice. On the remote Cassiar Highway, I almost hit a wolf that dashed in front of my truck, and in Clayoquot Sound, I watched a pair of young wolves scavenging in the intertidal zone. And that is it. Two decades contemplating wolves but perhaps only fifteen encounters in the wild.

Given the number of months I have spent in wolf country and the relatively few wolves I have seen, I estimate our chances of seeing a wolf in Yellowstone at about 5 percent. Even this meager percentage would seem wildly overoptimistic except that wolves are easy to see in Yellowstone, at least in comparison with other "wolfy" locations in North America. In an email exchange with Ed Bangs, one of the primary biologists associated with the Yellowstone wolf reintroduction, he said he thought our chances of seeing a wolf in Yellowstone in May were "quite good in the Lamar Valley"—the result of relatively high wolf densities, open countryside, and substantial road access. In Algonquin Park, where wolf density would be similar, the heavily forested landscape makes seeing wolves from a distance impossible except during winter, when they will occasionally venture onto frozen lakes. Because it is relatively easy to see wolves in Yellowstone, wolf biologists have learned a great deal about wolf behavior here, arguably more than has been learned in decades of research at other locations.

Gray wolves (*Canis lupis*) used to range across almost all of North America. But then, through a complicated blend of fairy tales dosed with a pinch of reality, wolves were portrayed as wanton killers of livestock and children. The persecution that resulted was remarkable in its efficiency. Throughout the nineteenth and twentieth centuries, hundreds of thousands of wolves were killed in the United States and Canada. Professional "wolfers," encouraged by pelt prices and bounties, employed all means available—bullets, traps, and poison—to kill as many wolves as possible. Extinction was the sanctioned goal, and that goal was almost achieved in the lower forty-eight states. National parks provided no safe haven—the wolves of Yellowstone were eradicated by 1926. By the 1950s, only a few remnant packs persisted south of the forty-ninth parallel.

For seventy years, the greater Yellowstone ecosystem suffered without any wolf packs. Then, in 1995, after years of debate, fifteen Albertan wolves gathered from a variety of packs were transplanted to Yellowstone's northern range. The following year, seventeen more wolves, this time from British Columbia, were transplanted. In both years, the wolves were reintroduced to the park via a slow release. The wolves were housed in large enclosures for a few months before they were allowed to roam free, an acclimatization period that helped prevent the wolves from wandering back home. The reintroduction was wildly successful, if controversial. The most recent wolf survey, from 2010, indicates that the park is home to a relatively stable population of about a hundred wolves split among eleven packs, though there have been quite a few more wolves in some years. This wolf reintroduction program is perhaps more appropriately termed a wolf acceleration program, however. Given the concurrent, natural expansion of wolf packs into Montana and Idaho from Canada, it is quite likely that wolves would have reached Yellowstone of their own volition, albeit a decade or more later than 1995.

From a scientific perspective, the most interesting aspect of the wolf reintroduction has been the impact of the wolves on other species in the greater Yellowstone ecosystem. Studies of this impact can take decades, but early data suggest the effects have been profound. Several studies now indicate that the return of the wolf is triggering an ecological ripple effect that is affecting the abundance and distribution of many other species, species that are often removed from the wolf by several links in the food web—a near-textbook example of what ecologists term a trophic cascade. Although such ecological linkages are hard to establish irrefutably, the data suggest that the wolves have influenced the abundance and distribution of elk, bears, cottonwoods, beavers, ravens, coyotes, trout, and grasses, among many other species.

The link between wolves and elk, which constitute the primary food source for most wolf packs in the park, is probably the strongest link. Since the early 1990s, elk numbers have been reduced by half. Grizzlies, which are too slow to regularly kill elk but powerful enough to take over most wolf kills, are benefiting from all of the extra protein in their diet—grizzly numbers are on the rise. The reduction in the overabundant elk has allowed the growth of cottonwood and willow saplings, none of which made it to maturity under the extreme grazing pressure that existed before the wolf's return. Beavers, which are occasionally eaten by wolves, are nonetheless reestablishing themselves in the park because they eat cottonwood and willow saplings. Ravens, magpies, beetles, and most other carrion scavengers are, like the grizzly, making good use of every wolf kill. Coyote numbers have been dramatically reduced through direct conflict with the wolves—they are no longer the top canid in this ecosystem. Trout and trout streams in general have benefited from the growth of streamside vegetation, which moderates temperatures and provides nutrients. Even the grasses have benefited because of changes in the foraging behavior of elk and bison.

Again, not all of these linkages have been firmly established via experimentation, but each year there are more supporting data and more hypotheses to test. Clearly, the impacts of this apex predator, a keystone species if ever there was one, are far-reaching. And the fact that wolf packs are now more or less continuous from Yellowstone to the Canadian border is a real conservation success story.

As a family unit, we drive back out to the road closure at the eight-mile mark. Things haven't changed at all, except the angle of the light—the road is still littered with shaggy bison. They still amble along nonchalantly, despite the vehicles creeping through the herd, literally within a few feet of some individuals. The bisons' breath billows and their haunches steam and their patties effuse, together releasing enough moisture to precipitate a herd-shrouding fog in the cool air. Since they weigh up to two thousand pounds each, it is perhaps not surprising that a three-hundred-strong herd of bison can create its own weather. Because we are only driving at about four miles per hour, we let Brora sit up front on Briana's lap so that she can get a good look at the bison, too.

We stop to hike a trail that loops south of the park road. Briana carries Finn in the Man Uterus, and I chase after Brora. The weather is perfect. The day is warming quickly and the sky is a perfect blue. The trail is lovely, too, snaking off through the grassland and then paralleling a little creek in the forest.

But I am too on edge to enjoy any of it. It is the damn grizzlies. They wrecked my sleep in Alaska, and now they are wrecking my first family hike in Yellowstone. I did not think about a grizzly once when I was hiking by myself this morning, except to hope that I would see one from a distance. It is the mix of kids and grizzlies that has me nervous—they seem a particularly bad mix.

I watch Brora running ahead of me, squealing with delight. She sounds like an injured animal, an elk calf with a broken leg. I hear Finn mewling behind me, a mewling that turns to crying, a crying that turns to screaming. His lungs must be the size of hot air balloons. Every grizzly in the northern range is perking its ears right now, smacking its lips, and tying a napkin around its neck.

Then I look back at Briana. Burdened with Finn, who is tucked completely inside her jacket for warmth, she looks seventeen months pregnant. She will not be able to run anywhere like that. Not that we are supposed to run, I recall; running could trigger a chase response. We are supposed to play dead. But how can anyone play dead when their kids are with them? I will need to be a decoy. I will have to lure the bear away and then play dead, which will be easy because I will be dead.

Then, as we near a picnic area along the creek, I see a sign posted on a tree: "Warning: A bear has been frequenting this area. Your safety is not guaranteed in bear country."

Well, this is fucking great, I think. Why would the park service not put the warning sign at the trailhead? The idiots have lured us into a trap—let's get the tourists a third of the way down the trail, and then we'll let them know that there's a bear guarding the route.

To my credit, I completely internalize my mounting panic.

"Now that we've come this far," I say nonchalantly, "we might as well keep going."

Briana looks up from cooing at Finn—she has not given the circling grizzlies one thought. Like changing a flat tire or taping drywall or investigating strange noises at night, worrying about grizzlies is solely my responsibility.

Then Briana asks me, "Should we stop for a snack?"

Have you lost your fucking mind? I almost shout, but instead I say, "If we want to see Old Faithful today, we'd better keep going."

A couple of German tourists have just passed us on the trail and, ever the altruist, I intend to use them as a human shield. Let them spring the trap.

Then Briana asks, "Can you at least take Finn?"

"Do you want to be the decoy?" I mumble.

"What?"

"Oh, nothing," I say. "Give me Finn."

Finn is about the size of a butterball turkey. Walking with him attached to my stomach is awkward because he eclipses my feet. Consequently, as I lumber along, I have to study the trail six feet ahead and pick my exact route two steps ahead of the current step. The actual placement of each foot requires faith, which is currently in short supply.

This is what life will be like all the time, I think, if I keep shoveling in those American-sized portions.

And with my fat man's eyes glued to the trail ahead, how can I scan for grizzlies? Plus, our human shield, the very fit and unburdened-by-offspring Germans, have left us in their dust. We are alone.

The trail climbs to a modest lookout, and we get good views to the south. There are big mountains and snow in the distance, but the nearby grassland is free of snow except in the deeper coulees. Dark bison randomly dot the landscape like glacial erratics.

The sun feels suddenly hot, and with Finn strapped to my front and the daypack strapped to my back, I start to sweat profusely. The wind is picking up, too, carrying my sweaty stink across the plain. I imagine the dusting of aromatic molecules we have left on the trail behind us, and I can almost see them blowing ahead of us in the billions. We are akin to an apple pie cooling on the windowsill of a house that is adjacent to a hobo village—there is little chance we will survive until dinnertime.

"It's gorgeous," Briana says, looking through her binoculars.

"Absolutely," I say, breathing deeply. "But we better get moving."

I say this quickly because I can tell Briana is about to sit down and contemplate the landscape. Briana looks at me, a little annoyed, but she starts walking again nonetheless.

Brora runs after Briana, but she is running out of steam. She stops and picks up a rock; three steps later she stops to exchange the rock for a stick. I follow along behind, eyes flicking between the trail and the forest.

Then I see it—a huge bear scat. It is curled up next to the trail like a two-foot section of kielbasa that has ruptured its casing. I borrow Brora's stick to poke it. The scat is fresh enough to still be glistening, though not fresh enough to still be steaming.

"Big poop," says Brora.

"Yes," I whisper, feeling the adrenaline surge that only grizzly scat of that size could elicit. "Why don't you ride on Daddy's shoulders?" I say, lifting her up. Then, feeling like an overburdened Sherpa, I start trotting after Briana.

When I catch up to Briana, I pass Brora to her.

"Keep her close," I say. Then I take the lead and start moving haphazardly down the trail at double time. The fast pace is unwise: I trip on a rock and stumble forward, catching myself with my hands. The Man Uterus ruptures and Finn launches halfway out into the world, a botched c-section of sorts. Jolted from sleep, he starts screaming wildly. I stuff him back in and pull the straps tight in an attempt to muffle the dinner bell.

Then, without losing more than a step or two, I keep going, albeit a little more carefully. Twice, I stop to wait for Briana and Brora to catch up—they are having a great time looking for rocks that are real keepers.

"Leave the rocks," I finally say in a tone that Briana understands.

I do not relax until I see the van glistening in the distance like a ruby. There are people mingling in the parking lot, and a string of cars is stopped on the highway. By the time we reach them, the commotion has died down.

An elderly man with a serious camera asks, "Did you see the grizzly?"

"No," I say.

"It ran across the highway maybe fifteen minutes ago."

"Did you get some shots?"

"No," he says. "I was too slow, but it was a big bruin."

We wait around with everyone else, hoping for the unlikely return of the grizzly. The wait gives me time to ponder the most stressful hike of my life. In a sense, the hike brings me closer to understanding why grizzlies were persecuted so fiercely, why they were driven back from early human settlements.

I never really understood this until Brora and I were hunched over that fresh grizzly scat and I knew there was a chance I would be faced with a situation in which I could not protect her. In contrast to the scenario in my nightmare, I know I would put myself between a grizzly and my family—but I also know that that might not be enough to save them. In that short three-mile hike, I truly felt the burden of fatherhood for the first time.

Grizzlies, like wolves, used to range across much of North America. California has a grizzly on its flag because it used to contain a lot of grizzlies. The Great Plains was also prime grizzly habitat. But by the early 1900s, as a result of persecution by humans, grizzlies were largely confined to remote mountainous regions of Canada and Alaska, and only a handful wandered the mountains south of the forty-ninth parallel. Somehow, a few persisted in the Yellowstone area, secluding themselves in the remotest valleys.

Then, in 1975, grizzlies in the lower forty-eight were officially listed in the Endangered Species Act. Since listing, there has been a gradual increase in their number. In 1975, there were an estimated 136 grizzlies in the greater Yellowstone ecosystem, and today there are almost 600. Their range has also been expanding: grizzlies are back in areas they have not occupied in a hundred years.

Some of the most interesting research on grizzlies in the Yellowstone area has been trying to determine an appropriate minimum viable population—the smallest population that still has a high probability of persisting over the long term. From a strict conservation perspective, more individuals spread across a larger range is always better, because the likelihood of inbreeding is reduced and the impacts of an environmental disaster, such as a massive forest fire, are less likely to be catastrophic. But with a species like the grizzly bear, given its large home ranges and sometimes disagreeable demeanor, the population cannot get too large—there is not enough suitable habitat and the potential for conflict with humans needs to be minimized. Yellowstone biologists are, therefore, faced with the difficulty of trying to ensure that the grizzly population remains viable while simultaneously minimizing human-bear conflicts.

So how many grizzlies are required to ensure their viability in Yellowstone? A rule of thumb that gets bandied about in such discussion is the 50/500 rule, which suggests that fifty breeding individuals are needed in the short term to avoid significant inbreeding and five hundred breeding individuals are needed long term to retain some ability to evolve as environments change. These numbers refer not to the total number of individuals but to the number of effective breeding individuals, which is typically a small subset of the total population. The 50/500 rule is universally criticized as being too general to be of any use—each species in each region needs its own management plan—but managers like it because it presents a clear target to strive toward while field biologist argue about the specifics.

An effective breeding population of five hundred grizzlies would likely necessitate a total population size of a couple thousand individuals to compensate for wonky sex ratios, immature individuals, and natural fluctuations in population size. Even for the greater Yellowstone ecosystem, which includes adjacent parks and national forests, this number may be unrealistically large because there simply may not be enough suitable habitat— a population of a couple thousand grizzlies would require a very large area indeed. Exactly because grizzlies demand a lot of land, they are one of the best examples of what conservation biologists refer to as an umbrella species. If enough habitat is protected to ensure a viable population of an umbrella species, other species that demand less land will also have viable populations within this large habitat. From a resource management perspective, umbrella species offer a straightforward way of assessing ecosystem integrity. A healthy, viable population of grizzlies in the Yellowstone area indicates that the whole system is in pretty good shape.

Despite being the most intact landscape south of the fortyninth parallel, the Yellowstone area may not be large enough to support a population of grizzlies that is truly viable in the long term. If this is the case, another way to help maintain a viable population is to ensure that movement corridors exist between the Yellowstone population and other populations to the north. Several nonviable populations can become viable if they are connected by corridors that allow the movement of individuals and thus their genes. Small populations that are linked have a much greater probability of persistence than either population in isolation.

The Yellowstone to Yukon Conservation Initiative (Y2Y) is a grand scheme along these lines. The goal of the initiative is to ensure that national parks and other core habitat in the mountainous regions stretching from Yellowstone to the Yukon are adequately connected. Such connectedness would, for example, allow grizzly bear genes to flow, over many generations, between Yukon and Yellowstone populations. Such vast connectivity would help ensure the long-term viability of many species, even in the face of landscape-altering threats such as climate change. If nothing else, forty years of conservation biology has shown that connectivity is good; isolation is bad.

That afternoon, we drive south through the park for an hour to see Old Faithful, the most famous geyser in the world. As we reach the parking lot, lovely Finn takes a nasty poop in, and out of, his diaper. Then, as we are preparing for the cleaning procedure, we realize that we have left all of the diapers in the cabin. Rather than concoct a diaper out of Kleenex and Saran Wrap, we decide to forgo Old Faithful and simply head back to the cabin—the overcrowded parking lot has soured my desire to see the old geyser anyway.

Wolf track

With fragrant Finn strapped back into his car seat, Briana drives us back to the cabin with the van windows down despite the near-freezing temperatures in this part of the park. She cannot drive very fast because the road conditions are still not great—a potentially deadly mix of slippery snow and massive bison.

We are perhaps two-thirds of the way back to the cabin, north of Norris but still well south of Mammoth, when Briana cries, "Wolf!"

I was busy entertaining Brora and Finn, but I turn in time to see a black wolf trotting along the left shoulder of the road. Briana pulls over and rolls to a stop, and then, directly in front of the van, the wolf cuts across the road and disappears into the forest. I grab the camera from the center console, jump out of the van, and run up to where it entered the forest, but it has disappeared into the thick spruce. I try walking a little way into the forest, but the snow is at least three feet deep, and I sink up to my crotch. The only pictures I get are of paw prints, but I return to the van jubilant nonetheless.

The total sighting lasted maybe fifteen seconds, which makes it longer than at least half of my wolf sightings. The wolf was mostly black but flecked with touches of gray or white on its chest and muzzle. Compared with other wolves I have seen, particularly the Algonquin wolves, which are quite small, this wolf, like all wolves in Yellowstone, was big. Females are typically around 100 pounds and males around 120 pounds, whereas Algonquin wolves are on average 30 pounds lighter. At the time of the reintroduction, one of the criticisms was that the wolves being reintroduced were extra-large Canadian wolves.

Briana is surprised that I am so excited by such a marginal sighting, but I don't think she realizes just how lucky we are. The sighting was even more unlikely because we are in a forested part of the park and not in open habitat like the Lamar Valley. Despite the relatively heavy traffic on the road, we were the only vehicle to see the wolf, which makes it even more special. Thanks to a poopy diaper and crappy packing, we just saw one of the species I was almost certain we would not see on this road trip.

The next morning, I again rise before dawn and head out on the north park road. Despite rumors to the contrary at the hotel, the road is still closed because of the mudslide. This is a real drag, because the famed Lamar Valley lies beyond the closure. The Lamar Valley is, in fact, completely cut off, because the Beartooth Highway, which enters the northeast corner of the park, is still closed as a result of the monumental snow pack. So again, I have to satisfy myself with the wildlife that clogs the first eight miles of road—elk, bison, pronghorn, mule deer—but no wolves or bears.

That afternoon, we pack more carefully and again drive south toward Old Faithful. En route, we stop to hike another trail—this time I try harder to enjoy myself and think less about grizzlies. It is probably the first time in my life that I am glad that a hiking trail is busy. There are large clumps of people both ahead of us and behind, which is comforting because research indicates that bears almost never attack large groups—a statistic Parks Canada makes use of by forcing people to hike in groups of six or more in areas where grizzly encounters are likely.

By the time we get to the Old Faithful parking lot, both kids are sound asleep.

Briana asks, "Do you really need to see Old Faithful?"

"Not at all," I say. And with that, Briana starts driving slowly back toward the cabin.

We are perhaps halfway back, somewhere south of Norris, when eagle-eyes Briana shouts, "Bear!"

I look to the road and sure enough there is a grizzly crossing just ahead of the car in front of us.

"Grizzly!" I shout.

Briana rolls to a stop on the shoulder while I snap off a few quick pictures before the bear disappears into the forest. Then I get out and walk along the highway, looking into the forest. And there it is—the grizzly has stopped maybe a hundred feet into the forest to chomp at some grasses in a marshy area. I take a few photos, just to confirm the sighting. The bear is largely obscured by foliage, but in the photos you can see that it's a grizzly. Then I race back to the van for the camera with the telephoto lens.

With the kids sleeping, Briana and I both grab a camera and each quickly take a hundred photos. The grizzly is moderately sized, neither a yearling nor an eight-hundred-pound behemoth. I would guess three hundred to four hundred pounds. The fur is classic grizzly, a lovely grizzled golden brown that is darker

brown on the shoulder hump and legs. The bear looks almost docile as it slowly moves through the treed wetland, eating grass and rolling logs to look for grubs.

The big telephoto lens sitting atop the tripod is like a stoplight on the highway. Every car that goes by stops and asks what we are looking at, and when they hear it's a grizzly, they just about poop their pants. Soon, there are ten

Grizzly bear

people lining the highway and ten cameras clicking away like guns at a firing range. And the growing crowd is a beacon that causes more and more people to stop.

Then, as I am walking back to the van to check on the kids, a second grizzly runs across the road, seemingly following the path of the first.

"Grizzly!" I shout. Everyone turns to look at the bear, and the bear turns its head toward me, a daunting gaze if ever there was one. After a long hibernation, its skin is sliding loosely over its big frame—this is a hungry bear. Then it disappears into the forest remarkably fast for a bear of that size. It is a quick sighting, but I am confident that the second grizzly is significantly bigger and that the coat is a much darker brown overall. I manage to take two quick photos, but the telephoto lens has such a small field of view that when I search the image after the fact, I learn that I missed the bear completely.

The first bear has doubled back toward the road and then meandered parallel to it, and I wonder if the second grizzly will follow the same path. I position myself among the people in the crowd, who are still watching the first bear, and wait for the second bear to reappear. I spend ten minutes waiting, taking occasional pictures of the first bear whenever I get a better view of it. The second bear never does reappear, but the crowd keeps growing. A tour bus stops, and twenty seniors stumble off. A string of fifty parked cars lines both shoulders, and more cars are stopped right on the highway. Within fifteen minutes of the original sighting, the scene has turned into a grizzly gong show.

The crowd of grizzly gawkers—and I realize I am one of them—sours my interest in watching this grizzly any longer. It has been a long time since I have observed wildlife in a mob like this, and I have forgotten how unpleasant it is. People jostle and toss elbows as they try to secure the best position to take the best crappy picture. Horns honk as drivers try to maneuver their cars next to the bear. The bear does not seem to care, but I do. And I feel responsible, because we started it—if we had not pulled over to take a picture of the bear, there is a good chance it would have moseyed along unmolested.

That night, I write in my journal that I would rather watch a song sparrow gather nesting material in my backyard than watch a roadside grizzly in the company of a mob like that. I am more convinced than ever that the only real wildlife sightings, the only ones that should really count, are those that happen when you are alone and well away from a vehicle. Of course, those sightings are hard to come by, particularly in an ecosystem that you do not know well and are just visiting for a brief moment with your young children.

We spend three more days in Yellowstone trying to get sightings of wolves and grizzlies that feel more real. Every morning before dawn, I head out alone, returning at pancake time. Then we set out as a family to view some attraction or hike or look for wildlife. After a family dinner on our cabin's porch, I might head out again until dark. We see a lot of wildlife, but the wolves and grizzlies remain elusive. We do manage to see two more grizzlies, but they are both roadside bears and no more real than the first. Unfortunately, the north road remains closed for the duration of our trip, so we never reach the Lamar Valley.

Overall, the Yellowstone portion of our trip ends up being a mix of beautiful and crowded—I cannot imagine the crowds in July and August. Nonetheless, I look forward to returning to the park in twenty years to see how the wolves have transformed it. Perhaps the regenerating forests will make the wildlife viewing poorer? Perhaps the grizzlies will be truly flourishing thanks to the wolves? Now that the grizzlies are on the road to recovery, I imagine their management will have to change. I would not sleep well if I were the grizzly biologist for Yellowstone—a thousand grizzlies and a few million visitors per year will guarantee a lot of conflict. Indeed, grizzly-human conflict already appears to be on the rise. Within a few weeks of our visit, two people were killed by grizzlies in Yellowstone Park in separate incidents. These were the first fatal grizzly attacks in the park since 1986.

very specific criteria that need to be met. At home, Briana is a largely vegetarian, totally organic, no-plastic-touching-her-food kind of girl. For the last decade, she has refused to eat anything cooked in a microwave. Beans should be soaked, not canned. Flour should be more chaff than grain. Milk, organic of course, must come in glass bottles. Granola is something you make before eating. Cane sugar, regardless of the hue, is a no-no, but organic honey or maple syrup can be used in minute quantities. Prepackaged foods of any sort—salad dressing, breakfast cereal, granola bars, ravioli, soup, etc.—are universally repugnant.

In truth, I have many of the same food preferences as Briana, but the gap between my good intentions and everyday actions is formidable, a veritable canyon of hypocrisy. (A similar canyon of hypocrisy also haunts my attempts at being a better environmentalist. Can an environmentalist really have kids, travel, eat mangos, own a house, or drive a car?) My modern intention to eat organic everything conflicts with my Scottish heritage. I find it almost impossible to pay more for a product that is seemingly of poorer quality—how many times have I bought organic produce that looked half as good as the conventional produce that cost half as much? Once, early in our relationship, Briana and I rode our bikes to the farmer's market to buy some organic veggies for a dinner we were hosting. Briana, a regular at the market, went right to her favorite vendor and proceeded to load up. For some reason, I insisted on paying, which was a mistake because when I heard the amount of cash I had to produce, I almost spit out the free cheese sample I was happily masticating. The very modest butternut squash alone cost ten dollars. I remember looking at Briana and wondering if this was a make-or-break moment in our relationship. If I walked away from this squash, would Briana walk away from me? Not wanting to take a chance, I forked over the thick wad of bills—thankfully I had just gone to the bank machine.

I recount that farmer's market story only to highlight the degree of stress I feel each day trying to feed the family—not in the traditional we-have-no-money sense but rather in the entirely modern there-is-no-organic-produce-anywhere sense. My one promise to Briana before the start of the trip was that I would try my best to feed her in her normal fashion. But, on the back roads of Middle America, I am failing miserably to keep this promise. While on the road, it might be okay to purchase toilet paper at Walmart but certainly not lettuce or bread. We have yet to find a gas station that stocks organic milk or organic bananas. The sorts of restaurants that line an interstate—typically the King, the Clown, and the Colonel—are obviously off limits, even in dire emergencies. But most of Middle America seems to offer almost nothing else. The landscape might be awe-inspiring, but the dining options are horrid. So whenever we get the chance to fill our moveable larder with finer foods, such as at the organic grocery store in Billings, we tend to overdo it.

Momentarily satiated, we head east out of Billings on the interstate but transition to a secondary highway as soon as possible. Our intent is to avoid the interstate highways whenever possible—they are efficient but always soulless. The road we choose this time is Route 212, which rolls through eastern Montana and, eventually, into South Dakota. After stopping to walk around the historical site of the Battle of the Little Bighorn, Custer's Last Stand, which is interesting and offers nice views of the surrounding grasslands, we continue east on the 212, the drooping sun at our backs. It has already been a long day, so we hope to find a campsite soon.

Route 212 is an utterly empty two-lane highway that runs straight as an arrow through some fine countryside—the population bomb clearly did not explode in eastern Montana. But it is without campgrounds or even motels of any sort. Then, after driving for more than an hour, we discover that the road is suddenly impassable because of a washout. Without any signage or even a usable map—the scale on our Auto Club map is suitable only for interstate travel—we really have no idea how to proceed. Because I am always opposed to backtracking, we decide to cut south and try to work our way around the closure. The detour takes us into the heart of the Northern Cheyenne Indian Reservation, where the road turns to gravel, dirt, and finally mud. We backtrack to a crossroads that has a few houses scattered about. We can see another car in the far distance approaching the intersection.

"Ask them for directions," I tell Briana.

"You ask," she says.

"You ask," I say.

"You ask," she says.

Finally, I grab Brora and get out of the van to wait for the other car to approach the intersection. I take Brora with me because I want to be seen as a family man in need of help and not some loner looking for trouble. But the car, loaded with teenage males, blows right past us and right through the faded stop sign without even a blink from the brake lights. We are still standing there somewhat agog when the next car rolls up and, remarkably, comes to a full stop. The driver, an older woman, rolls down her window.

"You folks must be lost," she says, and then provides impeccable directions around the washout.

By the time we get back on the 212, the sun has set. We are in the middle of nowhere, low on gas, and out of water, and of course the backseat screaming has begun.

"We should have stayed at a motel in Billings," I say.

"We should have stayed on the interstate," Briana says.

There is nothing to do but keep going. With only half a liter of water, we cannot even try to find somewhere to sleep rough, an option that I must admit seems a little terrifying on this dark night. So we keep going. Thankfully, the kids fall asleep relatively quickly, and I barrel down the empty 212, watching the fuel gauge slide past empty.

On fumes, we roll into the scrappy village of Broadus, and, thankfully, the only gas station is still open. There is a dilapidated motel here, too, but the motorcycles in front of each room make me hesitate. I ask the old guy working at the gas station about the motel, but he just shakes his head. So, refueled, we drive on.

It is well after midnight when I carry the kids, sound asleep, into a crappy but adequate motel in Belle Fourche, South Dakota. Three drunk, but friendly, nineteen-year-old girls carrying big dildos are in the motel hallway, and they tell us about their bachelorette party. Our friend is marrying a Marine tomorrow, they say, waving the dildos excitedly about.

Badlands National Park in South Dakota is most famous for its eroded cliffs, hoodoos, and pinnacles. But the park also contains one of the largest preserves of grassland habitat in North America, and we have planned a three-day stop primarily to spend some time in that endangered habitat. Because grasslands were easily converted to cropland or ranchland, almost every scrap on the continent was cut into sections and converted to farms by the 1920s. Tattered original remnants still remain, though these isolated scraps are often besieged by invasive plants and development plans. Other patches of previously modified grasslands are slowly being restored to a more natural state. In fact, restoration ecology as a discipline got its start partly through attempts to convert marginal farmland back into native grassland.

Black-tailed prairie dog

On gravel back roads, we drive around the park and enter from the south—yesterday's marathon drive has given us extra time for casual exploration. We are en route to the park's campground, but we cannot make it all the way there without first getting out of the van and running willy-nilly through the grasslands. We stop in the Conata Basin, just south of the primary mass of hoodoos, and walk/run as a family into the fine grassland habitat. The grass is knee-high on me but all the way up to Brora's forehead—from her perspective, the whole world is akin to a giant corn maze. Then, cartwheeling and somersaulting, we reach the prairie dog colony that we could see from the gravel road.

We sit quietly, at least as quietly as we can manage, and wait for the prairie dogs to reappear. Soon enough, we hear their whistles, and then we see them peeking out of their burrows. These are black-tailed prairie dogs (*Cynomys ludovicianus*), a threatened species in Canada and an important keystone species/ecosystem engineer across their range—many other species make use of their burrows, or the prairie dogs themselves, as prey. Several species that are also of conservation concern are associated with black-tailed prairie dogs—the badger, swift fox, burrowing owl, and black-footed ferret. The black-tailed prairie dog is the lynchpin that helps sustain each isolated scrap of grassland habitat.

The dog town is large, too large for me to estimate the number of burrow openings, though there are undoubtedly hundreds, perhaps thousands. The grass is cropped short within the colony, and a mound of dirt from tunnel excavation surrounds each opening. Several birds are making use of these modest mounds to survey the landscape; in a flat grassland, a foot-high mound of dirt surrounded by cropped grasses is the best perch from which to observe the surroundings. I see western meadowlarks, horned larks, and lark buntings, all of which seem to have an ecological relationship with the prairie dogs. Then, in the distance, I see a burrowing owl sitting on a mound, eyeing the landscape and us with vigilance.

Burrowing owls (*Athene cunicularia*) are, not surprisingly, owls that nest in burrows. They do not look a lot like a traditional owl, yet when I show Brora a picture of one in my bird book, she says "owl." So I guess they look enough like an owl. They are opportunistic feeders and will eat a variety of insects, small mammals, birds, snakes, and so on. Because they are dependent on scarce grassland habitat, they are in varying degrees of trouble across their range. For example, in British Columbia, which has a relatively small amount of grassland habitat, they were extirpated by 1950. A population has been reintroduced, but that population is not yet self-sustaining and needs continued management to persist.

But here in South Dakota, we are in their core range, and burrowing owls still seem common enough. I scan the dog town with the spotting scope and see four individuals without too much difficulty. I watch them watch us, and then I try stalking close enough to one to get a decent picture with the telephoto lens. But they are too wily for me and move smartly away whenever I breach some unseen perimeter. All I manage to take are a lot of bad pictures of burrowing owls, grainy-feathered lumps perched on the ground. The prairie dogs, however, are positively photogenic. Sit down twenty feet away from an active burrow, and within a few minutes a prairie dog will slowly emerge to whistle at you.

This landscape, the Conota Basin, is also the site of perhaps the most successful black-footed ferret reintroduction in the world. In the 1980s, black-footed ferrets (*Mustela nigripes*) were famous for being the rarest animal in North America and probably the rarest on the planet. Although the ferrets were not directly persecuted, they were completely dependent on prairie dogs. To eliminate perceived competition with livestock for forage, ranchers poisoned prairie dogs by the millions, shrinking and isolating dog towns that at one time were more or less contiguous across the Great Plains. The demise of the prairie dogs had direct and lethal implications for their predators, particularly the black-footed ferret, which was most strongly linked to the prairie dog. By the 1970s, the ferret was presumed extinct. Then, remarkably, in 1981, a ranch dog in Wyoming brought a dead ferret home to its owner, a bit of serendipitous hunting on the part of the ranch dog that resulted in the discovery of the very last colony of black-footed ferrets.

This last population of ferrets was small—less than a hundred individuals—and initially they were left in the wild. However, when this last colony was threatened by an outbreak of canine distemper, the last remaining ferrets, eighteen in total, were captured and a captive breeding program was started. Every black-footed ferret alive today is a direct descendant of those eighteen closely related individuals. Despite this incredibly tight genetic bottleneck and other risks associated with captive breeding, such as domestication, wild populations of ferrets are now established in the U.S., Mexico, and, recently, Grasslands National Park in southern Saskatchewan.

There are now about a thousand ferrets in the wild, spread among nineteen reintroduction sites, all of which are still very fragile in terms of population viability. The Conota Basin population is perhaps the most secure of an insecure bunch. In particular, the success of the Saskatchewan population is still in question because that site is at the northern limit of the ferret's historical range and black-tailed prairie dogs are themselves a threatened species in Saskatchewan. This is the sad reality of the modern grassland, where the persistence of an endangered species is dependent on the persistence of a threatened species—a precarious trophic pyramid, to say the least.

We decide to return to this dog town for sunset, when we will have a very slim chance of seeing a ferret. Ferrets are nocturnal predators and spend most of their time underground; consequently, our chances of seeing one in the wild are small. We'll also be looking for a swift fox (*Vulpes velox*), a species whose own history of unintended persecution and eventual reintroductions closely parallels that of the ferret, though the swift fox was never a baker's dozen away from extinction.

Because we are in a grassland, the campground does not afford any privacy. It is really just a bunch of picnic tables scattered around a relatively clean restroom, which is about all it can be, I guess. We pick a site as far away from the restroom and as deep into the grassland as we can manage. Then we make our standard spaghetti dinner with a side salad. The campground starts off pretty empty but fills up as dusk approaches—it is clearly a spot that people use for a night's rest en route to other locations.

The evening is perfect. The badlands can be a pretty nasty place—typically too hot or too cold. But today we're lucky. The high temperature for the day was about eighty degrees Fahrenheit, and there hasn't been a cloud in the big prairie sky. Like the Mojave, the badlands are hard to recommend for family camping, but if you get lucky with the weather, they are awesome.

We leave our campsite in time to reach the Conata Basin well before sunset. We park, leaving our own dog in the van, and walk out to the dog town. There we sit and wait on the off chance a black-footed ferret or swift fox will appear—though I have no idea why either species would come anywhere near our screaming and squealing corner of the dog town. Have I mentioned that young kids and wildlife viewing are somewhat incompatible? At least there are no grizzlies around to hear the dinner bell, and I'd match Brora against a badger or coyote any day. The prairie dogs, at least, seem immune to our commotion. They frolic and whistle and roll in the dirt and just generally carry on like kids at a day care.

Just before sunset, the mosquitoes appear in number, ravenous.

"I'll take the kids to the van," Briana says, "and give you a chance to see your ferret."

They amble off to the van, kicking up dog town dust the whole way. I walk farther into the dog town, trying to leave behind the area we so contaminated with our scent and sounds. I sit among some knee-high grasses on a little rise that offers good views of an especially busy part of the dog town. Then I slowly scan the landscape with my binoculars, watching prairie dogs pop up and down like a whack-a-gopher game.

Then, just as the sun drops below the horizon, the prairie dogs disappear for the night, seemingly all at once. My binoculars amplify the light a bit, and I can still see a burrowing owl in the distance. Then a coyote appears way off in the grasses, snaking its way toward me. But it cuts back into the grasses and disappears long before it gets anywhere near me. A meadow lark sings its last song of the day.

The western horizon is rimmed in yellow, which fades to deep purple higher up, the colors of an old bruise. In the east, stars appear in order of their magnitude. Then it is dark, too dark to see much of anything except the van glowing in the distance. I put my binoculars in my pack and walk back to the van, which is completely quiet with the kids asleep in the back.

The next morning, I get up in the dark and drive back to the Conata Basin to look for a ferret or fox. The sunrise is almost exactly like the sunset but reversed. The eastern horizon starts to glow, the birds start to sing, and then the prairie dogs appear all at once. A perfect dawn but no ferrets or foxes for as far as the eye can see.

I stroll through the long, wet grasses in my Wellington boots, surprised at the lushness and the amount of standing water. Clearly it has been a wet spring. These tall grasses, I think, will make it impossible to see a swift fox, which is about the size of a house cat. I was expecting the badlands to be more of a dust bowl. Then I crest a rise and startle a pronghorn, which bounds away as if it has mattress springs attached to each hoof. Boing boing boing!

Later that day, we move our camp to the more remote Sage Creek campsite, which is in a beautiful little valley. The campsite is rustic—vault toilets and no running water, except for

the lovely muddy creek, presumably Sage Creek, that runs right through it. The campsite is practically right on top of a dog town, which I hope will increase our chances of seeing a ferret or fox at some point.

In the late afternoon, two pickups pulling horse trailers roll into the campsite, and twenty minutes later, four horseback riders trot over the ridge. The riders are

Pronghorn

from Kansas and have just spent two days and nights on the open range. The horses are big and feisty, certainly not your average packhorses. And the riders really fit the Great Plains panorama—it's the first time I've ever seen anyone wearing cowboy boots and chaps who didn't look ridiculous. It takes them an hour to load up and leave us in the dirt, literally.

That night, we are the only people in the campsite, which makes for a truly perfect Great Plains experience. We spend the evening watching the dog town until the mosquitoes force us into the tent—at one point, little Finn has five mosquitoes on his perfect face. A full day in the fresh air, and everyone falls fast asleep in minutes.

During the night, I wake and walk out into the dog town by starlight. The stars overhead are spectacular—even the faint band of the Milky Way is visible, stretching across the sky horizon to horizon. It has been a long time since I've seen the Milky Way so clearly.

The next day is hotter. I feel the heat when I first get up to look for a ferret in the predawn. By midday we are looking for some respite, so we drive to the interpretive center for ice cream and the chance to refill our water jugs. I end up chatting with a knowledgeable park naturalist who is super keen on our family quest. He confirms that both the black-footed ferret and the swift fox will be very difficult to see, and he also confirms that the badlands have never been so green, at least not in his twenty years in the park.

"In a month," he says, "everything will be brown."

Back at the campsite, we go for a "rattlesnake walk" along the creek. Then we fill a big tub with water from the creek and let Brora play in that for the rest of the day. Briana finds a little shade and reads her book, while Finn sleeps in her arms. I just sit there and drink a few beers in the sun, one eye closed and one eye on the landscape.

The next morning I try to see a ferret or fox one last time, though by now I have convinced myself that just spending some time in their habitat is glorious enough. After a couple hours in the company of whistling prairie dogs and meadowlarks, I walk back to the campsite rejuvenated. Perhaps I am also mollified by the fact that there will be other chances on the trip, however slight, to see both species.

Back at the camp, I start loading the van under the beating badland sun—holy crap, is it going to be hot today. Brora runs around the campsite naked, and Finn sits in the dirt with a diaper on his head. Caked in mud from the creek, both appear to be on a quest for fire. Finally, van loaded and everyone fed, we dress the screaming kids and then strap them into their car seats. Our next scheduled species is the Kirtland's warbler in Michigan, but I am sure there are a few things to see between here and there.

EIGHT

twitching for
A RARE BIRD

"Birds are indicators of the environment.
If they are in trouble,
we know we'll soon be in trouble."
ROGER TORY PETERSON

After being on the road for six and half weeks, we run out of energy in Sioux Falls, South Dakota. Physically, we are smack-dab in the middle of the continent, 1,500 miles to either the Pacific or the Atlantic, and mentally, we are in the doldrums, suddenly pining for home and daunted by the thought of nine more weeks on the road. At the start of the trip, the sense of adventure outweighed the burden of travel, but suddenly, we are missing the familiar bed, top-notch barista, *Toopy and Binoo*, friends and family—even work is starting to look good after several weeks on the road.

Today, as we raced away from Badlands National Park, the outdoor temperature reached 102 degrees Fahrenheit, according to the minivan's built-in thermometer. It is our first taste of serious heat, and we don't like it. Briana, who has lived her whole life within biking distance of the cool Pacific, feels the heat the most and mopes around under her wide-brimmed hat like Paddington Bear. I knew we'd hit hot weather, but I wasn't expecting temperatures like this, at least not until Florida.

The heat forces us indoors. Instead of a picnic, we try eating at our first Perkins.

"Didn't Tiger Woods sleep with a Perkins waitress?" I ask Briana.

"How could Tiger be a Perkins regular and not weigh, like, four hundred pounds?" Briana asks. A good question given the amount of hollandaise sauce I've shoveled into my piehole.

Instead of camping under the stars, we hide from the heat in a crappy motel room. Brora and I suit up and head for the pool—it was the billboard on 190 highlighting a "Huge Water Park!" that tricked us into stopping at this motel. The water park is actually a pool with a slide, and it is closed. Apparently, some lovely child left a floater in the shallow end, and now the whole pool needs to be shocked with chlorine.

The next day starts like a case of gonorrhea—burning hot and itchy. Given the heat, there is nothing to do but drive. We stagger across the bottom of Minnesota, watching the vast wheat fields shimmer in the heat. Briana doesn't really like the landscape, but I can look at fields of wheat all day. I think of the size of the vegetable garden in our backyard, maybe sixty square feet, in contrast to the acreage stretching to the horizon, and a food shortage seems momentarily inconceivable. Eventually, we cross the Mississippi River, and then spend the night in yet another crappy motel, this one in La Crosse, Wisconsin. Rather than eat out again, I make dinner in the motel bathroom. This is not a good idea.

It isn't until we reach Michigan's Upper Peninsula that the heat dissipates; where the highway skirts Lake Michigan, the minivan's thermometer reads a perfect seventy-five degrees Fahrenheit, but whenever the road veers inland, the thermometer climbs into the mid-nineties—a twenty-degree lake effect. We camp right on the shore, skipping stones into what, from our shoreline perspective, might as well be the Pacific.

There is only one problem with the otherwise lovely campground: it is infested with ticks and littered with brochures about Lyme disease. At some point, I think Brora has a piece of food on her cheek, but it is a goddamn tick, just starting to dig in. Then I find one on my thigh. WTF? We seal ourselves in the tent, take off our clothes, and check everyone's cracks and crevices, particularly those of little Finny, which seem more delicate than ours do.

The next day, we drive east along the north shore of Lake Michigan and eventually cross into the Lower Peninsula via the Mackinac Bridge. Then we drive down I75 to a campsite near Grayling, Michigan. We are here to see a Kirtland's warbler, the rarest songbird in North America. The task of finding one of these rare birds is greatly simplified by the fact that the U.S. Fish and Wildlife Service offers free "Kirtland's Warbler Tours" every morning during breeding season (May 4 to July 4)—the free tours are an attempt to keep birders from trying to find the warblers on their own, a free-for-all that could potentially disturb nesting activity. To join one of these tours, all I have to do is arrive at the Ramada Inn in Grayling by 7 AM and look for the folks with the expensive binoculars.

Despite a middle-of-the-night thunderstorm, I manage to stagger out of the tent at 6 AM. Heavy gray skies loom, but the rain has stopped, at least for the moment. I leave everyone—wife, kids, and dog—sleeping soundly and drive for twenty minutes to the Ramada. Remarkably, given the rather remote location and the fact that it is the middle of the week, eleven birders have gathered there, sipping gas station coffee and chirping quietly about our chances of seeing a Kirtland's.

"If it rains," someone mutters, "we'll be screwed."

Luckily, today's tour guide is biologist Dan Elbert, a longtime coordinator of the Kirtland's warbler recovery project—the intern who normally does the tours has the day off and the boss is covering the shift. Before heading out into the field, Dan reviews the basics of Kirtland's warbler (*Setophaga kirtlandii*) biology. Through the 1970s and 1980s, Kirtland's numbers bottomed out at around two hundred singing males—literally a bad storm away from extinction. This small population was also very localized; almost every breeding pair could be found in the forests near Grayling.

Intensive research determined that two primary factors were causing the decline of the Kirtland's warblers: a lack of suitable nesting habitat and brood parasitism by brown-headed cowbirds. Large stands of young jack pine, pines that are five to twenty years of age, are required for successful nesting. Historically, forest fires created this type of habitat by burning mature forest and opening space for jack pine regeneration—jack pine cones typically release their seeds only after a forest fire, and their seedlings often dominate recent burns. By the 1980s, young jack pine stands were rare in Michigan, because forest fires had been successfully suppressed for more than fifty years.

Brown-headed cowbirds were also a major problem for Kirtland's warblers. Cowbirds are brood parasites, which means that they lay their eggs in the nests of other birds—a very cool reproductive strategy unless you're the host. The unsuspecting host, the Kirtland's warbler in this case, incubates the cowbird's egg and then raises the cowbird chick, often in lieu of raising any chicks of its own. Historically, cowbirds were birds of the open prairie, but human modification of the landscape allowed cowbirds to colonize most of the continent. Because Kirtland's warblers were not historically exposed to cowbirds, they did not evolve any defensive responses to brood parasitism. Thus, Dan quietly insists, cowbird populations needed to be reduced if the Kirtland's warblers were going to persist.

Kirtland's warbler

After Dan's presentation, everyone hustles out to their cars and we follow Dan, caravan-style, to the nesting habitat fifteen minutes east of Grayling. We abandon the vehicles and walk into the scrubby jack pine forest (and a swarm of black flies). Immediately, Dan's ears are twitching. "There's a palm warbler singing," he says, pointing, "and a clay-colored sparrow."

Dan describes this stand as perfect Kirtland's warbler habitat—nine-year-old jack pines with scattered open areas. "This young stand was created through a combination of harvesting and planting," he says. "Using controlled burns would be ideal, but they put people and property at risk."

No one is really listening to Dan; everyone is twitching to see a Kirtland's.

We continue walking into the jack pines. Dan points— a Kirtland's is singing in the distance. We walk some more. A man in a Tilley hat shouts that he sees one, but it quickly scuttles back into the brush before the rest of us can get a look. We hear another one only yards away, and Dan advises us to wait for this one to appear. It doesn't. We repeat this procedure again at the next birdsong. No luck. Finally, our persistence pays off—a glorious male perches briefly atop a little jack pine and belts out a clear chip-chip-che-way-o. Cameras click; birders sigh.

After seeing several more individuals, though none so clearly as the first, we head back toward the cars, stopping at a cowbird trap en route. The trap is basically a room-sized lobster trap—easy to get into and hard to get out of. The trap is baited with millet and seeded with a few live cowbirds.

"We kill about four thousand cowbirds a year," Dan says, "an unfortunate but necessary job."

A lady from Sweden asks, "How do you kill them?"

"We break their necks," Dan says. "It's quick."

I scan the group, expecting someone to protest this drastic measure, but no one seems at all ruffled by the killing of one species to save another. I guess we are all happy that we still have the chance to see a Kirtland's warbler. Everyone on this tour has seen scads of cowbirds, but without intensive intervention the Kirtland's warbler likely would have joined the ranks of the great auk and the passenger pigeon.

NINE

my old stomping
GROUNDS

"When you form relationships
with people from other nations, you accumulate
love miles: the distance between
your home and that of the people you love
or the people they love."
GEORGE MONBIOT, *Heat: How to Stop
the Planet from Burning*

The endangered species road trip eventually brings me back to my childhood home in southwestern Ontario. I return, as always, with the guilt of having left in the first place, of having abandoned ageing parents and young nephews to fend off the wolves without me.

We cross into Ontario at the Sarnia border crossing, with the red dirt of the Dakotas still clinging to our wheel wells. We aren't expected at my parents' house until the following night, but we're close and another night at a roadside motel is less than appealing. So I call ahead and ask if we can start our visit a day early—my parents are old enough now, late seventies, that a surprise pop-in would be too much. Given the hesitation in my mom's voice, it sounds like even arriving one day early is too much.

"We haven't gone grocery shopping yet," she says. "There's nothing for dinner."

We eat dinner on the road and arrive at 8 PM. Looking frailer than ever, my parents greet us in the driveway.

"Did you have dinner yet?" my mother asks worriedly.

"Yes," I say. "We had a nice dinner in London."

Finn is screaming like a little madman, Brora is running for the street, and the dog is growling at my father.

"That's quite a dog you got there," my dad says.

"Did you have dinner yet?" my mother asks again.

Our plan is to spend ten days in Ontario, where I will try to see a few endangered species—the wood turtle, American chestnut, and eastern prickly pear cactus. Plus, I have an appointment to tour the captive breeding facilities at the Toronto Zoo, which has been instrumental in saving Vancouver Island marmots and black-footed ferrets from extinction. But the Ontario leg of the road trip is primarily about giving my parents a chance to spend some time with their newest grandkids.

For me, it promises to be a tough visit—observing my parents' ageing bodies and suddenly forgetful minds leaves me utterly depressed. Forget the endangered species: I should be repairing the rotting deck, the sagging cupboards, the dripping faucets. I should be grocery shopping, cooking dinners, and driving my mother to her doctor's appointments. And, typically, this is exactly what I do on the first few days of my annual visit in an attempt to rectify a year of negligence. But by day four of each visit, I start wondering why I thought I would need to spend two weeks at my parents' house when a long weekend would have sufficed.

Later that night, I lie in bed with Brora, frustrated that I can't get her to sleep even though it is almost midnight, an hour that horrifies my parents, who think all kids should be in bed at seven and asleep by a quarter past. But Brora napped for three hours in the van today, and she ate enough brownies to sweeten her blood supply for a week. Eventually, after ten books and a lot of screaming, she falls fast asleep, going from full throttle to deep torpor in a millisecond. I remain lying there with one arm wrapped around her, too depressed to sleep but too exhausted to get up.

This visit is particularly depressing because of my parents' health. There have been health scares before, serious ones, but this time it's different. Whenever my sister's number appears on my call display back at home, I can actually feel my heart rate increase by 50 percent—is this the call? I'm depressed for my parents, who are experiencing the decline in health firsthand; I'm depressed for my sister, who will get stuck with a lot of the day-to-day work; and I'm depressed for myself, because I know I'm facing a great deal of guilt and many cross-country trips back to Ontario to pack boxes and consult with doctors.

Traveling by air to visit loved ones contributes to what George Monbiot aptly refers to as "love miles," which present a difficult and truly modern dilemma for those of us in far-flung relationships. I know it is immoral to regularly fly across the country, because flying is one of the major contributors to climate change. But is it not also morally wrong to not visit my immediate family, particularly when someone's health has taken a nosedive? Forced to choose between decreasing my carbon footprint and visiting my ailing mother, I'm afraid I'll be repeatedly stuck in economy class and contributing to the contrails over Saskatchewan.

The next day, my sister's family comes for a visit and the two of us discuss, in the basement, possible scenarios: in-home care, downsizing, and long-term care facilities.

"Sixty might be the new forty," I say, "but eighty will always be eighty."

"At least you're in Vancouver," she says. "You've got a 2,500-mile buffer."

"The love miles," I say, "are really going to swell my carbon footprint."

The conversation sends me repeatedly to my father's well-stocked liquor cabinet. By dinnertime, I'm slurring my way through the lasagna.

After three days of intensive family time, I need to get away, and searching for an endangered wood turtle provides the perfect excuse to get out of Dodge. I ask Briana if she and the kids want to come along, but she prefers to hang out at my parents' house (or more likely she prefers not driving anywhere for a while). Besides, she is somewhat oblivious to the growing tension between me and my father, and thus she is having a perfectly relaxing vacation. So that is how I find myself driving north, with only the pooch for company, for what will be my first night away from the family since Finn was born.

When I started my biology career in the early 1990s, one summer of field research in Algonquin Provincial Park turned into five more years and, eventually, a graduate degree. Even nowadays, when I dream of landscapes—which, trapped in my urban existence, I do a lot—the dreams are often of that rolling Canadian Shield: the silhouettes of white pines, the blazing orange of sugar maples in fall, and the sound of wolves howling on a winter night.

During my years in Algonquin, I caught and tagged and sometimes tracked a variety of species, and one of these species was the endangered wood turtle. The wood turtle project was a side project of my graduate supervisor, Ron Brooks, and thus it was a side project of mine. A typical day of wood turtle research during nesting season involved driving out to a known nesting location in the late afternoon and then waiting around for a turtle to climb out of the water and lay its eggs. After the turtle was done nesting, we would have to catch her before she slid back into the water and disappeared. Then, having caught the turtle, we would dig up the clutch of eggs and measure both the eggs and the female. If the female hadn't been previously caught, we would mark her by notching her shell and attaching a metal tag. The research not only helped to monitor the faltering wood turtle population but also identified changes in reproductive investment over an individual's life, among other things. Having now caught and tagged many species, I now think turtles are particularly great to work on because they seem quite agreeable to human handling. Contrarily, I am now reluctant to condone or participate in the netting and banding of birds, the trapping and tagging of mammals, or the marking of amphibians by clipping a unique series of toes, unless the questions being posed by the researchers are truly pressing.

Wood turtles (*Glyptemys insculpta*) are handsome turtles. They have a tan, nicely domed shell with prominent scutes and a strikingly yellow bottom shell called a plastron. The skin on their legs and neck is yellowish or sometimes reddish. Like most turtles, they are aquatic omnivores, but in contrast to their close relatives, they have terrestrial tendencies—in summer, they are sometimes found quite far from a water source. Although wood turtles still occupy a large geographic range, from the

Atlantic to Wisconsin, they are in serious trouble right across that range. In Ontario, there are three remnant populations, but each population is small and isolated. It is quite probable that the species will be extirpated from the province within the next few decades, if not globally extinct in the wild.

From my parents' house, it takes me five hours to get close to the wood turtle site, which is east of Algonquin Park proper. Then I get lost. It has been fifteen years since I was last at this site, and either things have changed or my mind has lapsed or both. I spend an hour racing around on a series of logging roads before I give up and return to the highway to buy a topographic map at a local gas station. The topo map illuminates my navigational error, and I race back into the forest, this time turning down the correct logging road. Soon enough, having driven as far as the Grand Caravan can manage, I park and Adie and I walk the rest of the way to the river, the banks of which offer a series of potential nesting sites.

The walk stirs memories of wood turtles. Actually, the memories are stirred by the biting insects—a near-lethal mix of mosquitoes, black flies, deerflies, and horse flies. This research location always had a lot of deerflies in particular, nasty little bastards with the bite of a pit bull, and nothing has changed in that regard. Plus, I have forgotten the insect repellent, but I recall that even the now-banned 95 percent DEET repellents, which I used to slap on like Aqua Velva, didn't impede the deerflies. Adie, a tough little dog, has clearly never seen biting insects like this; she snaps at them without effect and then runs helter-skelter down the trail. I zip up my Gore-Tex jacket, seal the cuffs, and pull up the hood—despite the fact that the air temperature is ninety degrees Fahrenheit and the humidity undoubtedly 80 percent. But it should be a good turtle evening—they always liked to nest on the hot, humid evenings, and the number of nesting turtles seemed to correlate with the number of deerfly bites. If your face wasn't a mess of welts by the time you reached the site, it was going to be a quiet night.

As we approach the nesting sites, I put Adie on a tight leash to keep her from disturbing any turtles. Each nesting site is at a sandy portion of the riverbank—the turtles climb out of the river and up the riverbank, dig a hole in the sand, lay a clutch of eggs in the hole, backfill the hole, and then slide back into the river. The eggs are then left to develop without any further parental investment, and if all goes well, tiny little turtles will hatch within a few months. However, the eggs are supremely vulnerable to a host of threats, especially the ubiquitous raccoon, which is a scourge to turtle eggs almost everywhere. If the hatchlings actually manage to survive their first decade, they then, like most turtles, have relatively low mortality rates and consequently long life spans of up to forty years in the wild. The primary risks to adult turtles are a result of humans: habitat loss, vehicle strikes, and collection for the illegal pet trade.

The biggest change in the local environment over the past fifteen years is the significant tree growth along the riverbank, which now provides ample shade to the sandy nesting areas. I imagine the tree growth will eventually ruin this nesting site, because without direct sun on the riverbank, the eggs may be too cold to finish developing before the summer wanes. But I see wood turtle tracks right away; they are quite obvious in the soft sand. I erase the tracks with my foot so that I won't get confused—if there are more tracks here when I return later, I will know they're fresh.

We continue walking along the riverbank, stopping to investigate each potential nesting area. We see more tracks and a couple of nests that have been ripped open by predators. Then, at a historical hot spot, I see a wood turtle at the base of the river-bank, still glistening wet. I stand motionless and then slowly start backing up, pulling Adie with me. Turtles that have just emerged are most sensitive to disturbance—once they have dug a deep hole, they are hard to scare off, but a turtle that has just emerged is likely to dive back into the river at the slightest disturbance.

I intend to give the turtle about forty-five minutes alone, enough time for her to commit to nesting. Then, once she is laying eggs, I can sneak close enough for a decent photograph. The last time I took a picture of a wood turtle, it was with a crappy film camera. So we walk back along the riverbank and recheck the earlier locations. Then we find a quiet spot to sit down by the river—it really is beautiful. I let Adie off the leash to give her a chance to frolic while I sit down on a rock and listen to the deerflies pelting off my jacket—sort of like listening to a hail-storm on a tent. Above the din, I can hear two white-throated sparrows singing behind me and a veery directly across the river. It has been fifteen years since I've heard either distinctive song, but they are impossible to forget.

After twenty minutes, we head slowly back toward the tur-tle, stopping to listen to birds en route: American robin, winter wren, red-eyed vireo, hermit thrush, yellow warbler, and black-throated green warbler—plus a few other species I can't identify high in the canopy. Each song triggers an Algonquin memory, a recollection of a time in my life when I was biologically over-whelmed by hundreds of new species and thoughts of their interconnections. The birds also remind me just how little bird-ing I've done on this trip. Whenever the kids are in tow, I feel too harried to bird. They force me to be more engaged with life in so many ways, but they inhibit careful wildlife observation or thoughtful contemplation of a landscape. This solo journey has given me a chance to do both.

The first turtle sites are still empty: no turtles and no tracks. Then, as we approach the spot where we saw the turtle, I tie Adie to a tree and get my camera out of the daypack. I walk forward on tippy toes, but when I get to the turtle spot, there is no turtle. From the tracks, it appears that the turtle explored halfway up the riverbank before returning to the water. There is a chance we spooked it when we first walked up, but we were quiet and didn't get within a hundred feet. I would guess that the turtle is still a day or two away from nesting, and it was just giving this site a prenesting look. But who the hell knows what a turtle is thinking?

We continue checking the length of the riverbank until well past sundown, but we don't see any more turtles. Then we start walking back toward the van. My plan is to sleep in the van tonight and then recheck the nest sites shortly after dawn. Although wood turtles are more likely to nest in the evening, there is a chance one will nest in the early morning, too. By the time we reach the forest, it is dark. "As long as we don't stray from the sound of the river," I tell Adie, "we shouldn't get lost." The trail cuts through a swampy area, and the frogs are deafening, a veritable cacophony of green frogs, gray tree frogs, American toads, and a few late spring peepers—the feel is more bayou than boreal. The insects continue to swarm, too, and with my hood up, my peripheral vision is completely compromised, which makes me feel extra vulnerable.

Thank goodness for intrepid Adie, who follows the trail with ease (at least I assume it's the correct trail). I really thought she was going to be trouble on this trip—we brought her primarily because she would be impossible to leave with anyone—but she has been a great addition in every landscape. And she loves spending twenty-four hours a day in our company, sleeping outside, lying between the kids' car seats, and eating whatever we are eating. We find the van without incident. I decide to drive back a few miles to a more scenic location along the river, where an old skidder trail creates a little pullout. I park, fold the backseats into the floor, and roll out my mattress and sleeping bag. When I was looking for a used minivan for the trip, the Dodge Caravan was attractive for two reasons. First, it was significantly cheaper than other minivans, and second, the backseats fold easily into the floor, leaving a flat surface that is perfect for sleeping on. If we weren't lugging around so much gear, the whole family could have easily slept in the van. Tonight, the only problem is that it is about a hundred degrees Fahrenheit inside the van, and if I open a window even a millimeter a million mosquitoes zoom in. Thankfully, an old friend with a lot of road trip experience convinced me to take along a piece of old window screen and some duct tape. So I tape a big piece of screen onto the frame of one of the side windows, and then open the window. Fresh air and no bugs!

Then Adie and I curl up on the floor of the van and listen to the gurgle of the river and the insects banging against the screen.

I want to say I slept terribly without my family snuggled close, but I sleep like a proverbial rock. Adie barked at something in the middle of the night, but I was too tired to even get up and take a look—I guess my fear of marauding bears or hillbillies is lessened when I don't have a family to protect.

By six o'clock, we are again trolling the riverbank in search of turtles. On first pass, there aren't any turtles nesting, and there are moose and raccoon tracks aplenty but no fresh turtle tracks since last night. So, again, we sit by the river listening to birds. A broad-winged hawk circles overhead, a belted kingfisher rattles past, an osprey searches the river for breakfast, and a great blue heron takes to the air with a prehistoric squawk. When I am seventy, long retired, with kids dispersed, I want to spend another year in this landscape. It will be interesting to see how much or how little it will have changed in the intervening fifty years since I first tromped these woods.

We walk along the riverbank until ten o'clock, looking everywhere for another turtle—in the river, on the bank, and even in the woods. I contemplate phoning Briana and asking whether I can spend another night here, but I am too worried about the dynamic at my parents' house. So, by noon, we are driving south with only the briefest wood turtle sighting to justify a five-hundred-mile round-trip.

By three o'clock, we are stuck in the horrible Toronto traffic. When you are stuck on Highway 401, in the middle of twenty horrifying lanes of traffic, you can't imagine any possible way that the planet will survive another century. Soon it seems everywhere will be paved and everything green will be dead.

The next couple of days at my parents' house are easier—everyone is getting into a groove. Even my father has chilled now that Finn will sit in his lap without screaming. The two of them sit in his big recliner for fourteen hours a day, both of them fast asleep for most of it. My mother totters around after Brora, who is on her best behavior. Briana reads her books in the shade. I find a couple of minor maintenance projects to keep me busy and make me feel better about myself, and I also find a couple of old high school friends to drink beer with.

Then Adie and I escape again for half a day to go see an American chestnut in the Deep South—of Ontario, that is. I take side roads all the way, cutting across a good chunk of Carolinian Canada, a term Canadians use to describe the deciduous forests of southern Ontario that share many similarities with forests as far south as the Carolinas. Here, the forests contain native trees that seem exotic for a country swathed in black spruce—tulip trees, butternut, black walnut, red mulberry, and even a few remnant American chestnut trees. Carolinian Canada is also home, albeit a tattered one, to many species that are at risk in Canada.

My destination today is the town of Aylmer, a farming community only ten miles from the shores of Lake Erie. Historically, this region grew a lot of tobacco and was prosperous as a result, but the region's decline is apparent as I drive past a lot of run-down or boarded-up farmhouses. In Aylmer, I meet a volunteer with the Canadian Chestnut Council, Ron Casier, who doubles as a retired high school science teacher. I follow him out to the council's test plot fifteen minutes east of town. The test plot acreage, a small corner of the large Riverbend Farm, was donated by the landowner and is managed by a handful of volunteers. The goal of the Canadian Chestnut Council is to reintroduce American chestnut trees across their native range in Canada.

Until the early 1900s, the American chestnut (*Castanea dentata*) was found throughout eastern deciduous forests, ranging from Georgia to Ontario. They were big, fast-growing hardwoods and, consequently, an important timber tree. They also produced a lot of nuts annually and were consequently an important food source for wildlife and humans alike. They were also numerous, comprising perhaps a quarter of the canopy trees across much of their range. In Ontario alone, there were millions of them, and throughout their core range in the United States, there were an estimated 4 *billion*. Then, in the early 1900s, a fungal pathogen from Asia, chestnut blight, was introduced via some transplanted Chinese chestnut trees or lumber products. The pathogen devastated American chestnut populations, which for some reason had almost no resistance, despite having been a large, vigorous population beforehand. Within a few decades, almost every single mature tree was dead. Interestingly, the rapid demise of the American chestnut, a very common and eco-logically dominant species, didn't trigger a massive trophic cascade. Undoubtedly, many species were negatively affected, but the loss of the chestnut did not result in the extinction of any bird species, for example, which were already quite well surveyed by 1900. Perhaps ecosystems are more resilient than we might imagine.

American chestnut

Despite the lethality of the fungal pathogen, the American chestnut didn't become extinct, but then it is often easier for conservation biologists to prevent the absolute extinction of plants than of animals. One reason for this is that plant con-servation biologists can insure against absolute extinction by storing seeds long term for later germination. The most famous seed bank is the Svalbard Global Seed Vault, which is located in the Norwegian Arctic and preserves millions of seeds from a wide variety of agricultural and wild species in case of a global catastrophe. I imagine there are some American chestnuts stored there, as well as at other North American seed banks. Additionally, plant conservation biologists can transplant asexual propagants to other locations; for example, a small number of transplanted American chestnuts persist in blight-free areas such as the Pacific Northwest.

A very small number of American chestnuts also persist in the wild across their native range, where surviving underground root systems still regularly send up new shoots. These young shoots grow into saplings, but the blight, which is still present in these ecosystems, typically kills the saplings before they have a chance to produce flowers and thus seeds. However, from these new shoots or few remaining trees, cuttings can be acquired. These cuttings can be grown and manipulated in nurseries, and any saplings that show some innate resistance to the blight can be selected for further propagation. The Canadian Chestnut Council is trying to do exactly that in the test plot at Riverbend Farm—grow saplings, inoculate these saplings with blight, and then select those saplings that have the most innate resistance for further propagation. The hope is to get a tree that retains the characteristics of the original—a tall, straight lumber tree—but with much greater resistance to the blight.

At Riverbend Farm, Ron and I walk through the test plot, which contains several hundred saplings of various heights. The ones planted last year are a foot tall, and the largest are perhaps twenty-five feet tall. I find it strange to walk among a grove of seemingly vigorous saplings and contemplate the fact that they are globally endangered. A number of them are even flowering.

Then Ron shows me the blight on the saplings, which looks rather innocuous at first glance—a little orangish rust on the bark. The rust, he explains, will turn to cankers, and the cankers will cause the bark to split, exposing the tree to other diseases and inhibiting the transport of fluids. By the time most of the trees have a trunk diameter of four inches, they will be dead or on their way to it. A few of the trees here managed to produce nuts last year, Ron says, but only a few.

Ron also talks about the great chestnut controversy. (It seems there is controversy everywhere, even between lovely people like Ron and his chestnut buddies.) Among those interested in restoring the American chestnut to its former glory, there are two camps—the all-American camp and the multiregional hybrid camp. The goal for both camps is to once again have the majestic chestnut dominating the canopy of eastern hardwood forests. But to achieve this end, the all-American camp wants to retain a pure American-only strain, whereas the other camp believes an American/Chinese hybrid will have a greater chance of success. The American and Chinese chestnuts are very closely related but differ significantly in morphology; the Chinese chestnut is spindlier and misshapen but, importantly, has much greater resistance to chestnut blight.

Both camps face difficulties. The all-American camp needs to select for resistance from within the much-diminished American chestnut gene pool, resistance that may not exist. The American/Chinese hybrid camp needs to incorporate the resistance of the Chinese chestnut while simultaneously retaining the larger, straighter morphology and tastier nuts of the American chestnut. The Canadian Chestnut Council is hedging its bets by trying both strategies—many of the saplings at this test plot are hybrids.

After touring the test plot and talking chestnuts for an hour, we meet Murray Alward in a greenhouse that contains a variety of native tree seedlings. Murray is the manager of Riverbend Farm and, according to Ron, the driving force behind the successes at the test plot. Murray is a farmer, but like most farmers, he is also part scientist and is always trying to solve some real-world problem using experimentation and a lifetime's worth of practical experience. To deal with the problem of blight, Murray performs testcrosses in his spare time, like a modern-day Mendel. I can barely follow the discussion that erupts between Murray and Ron about inoculations and virulence.

Then, after a five-minute lecture on testcrosses, Murray asks Ron, "Have you shown him the trees in the woodlot?"

"We were heading that way when we saw you," Ron says.

We walk over to the woodlot, stopping to look at a few more chestnut saplings that Murray has transplanted around the property. The woodlot is thick with overgrowth along the edges. Thirty feet in, Murray stops and points to a tree, a chestnut that is maybe a foot in diameter and encroaching on the canopy.

"I'm not sure of this tree's exact pedigree," Murray says, "but it's a heck of tree."

"How long before the forests are again full of trees like that?" I ask.

"We hope to have a suitable candidate for widespread planting within a decade," he says, "but it will take a couple of centuries before the forests again have a lot of chestnuts."

Farmers, I think to myself, are a patient bunch.

On the drive back to my parents' house, I zigzag through Carolinian Canada on a series of farm roads. The landscape is a lovely mix of farms and woodlots, truly the best of southern Ontario. For me, it's a hopeful drive through the landscape of my childhood. Hopeful because I know there are a lot of fine people like Ron and Murray working in their spare time to restore this landscape. Hopeful also because the landscape is clearly resilient and even modestly rewilding—southern Ontario's large population base has heaped a lot of abuse upon this landscape, but now I believe there is a chance that Carolinian Canada will survive with most of its species intact. When I last really explored this area fifteen years ago, I thought it was doomed for sure.

On the drive, my thoughts also wander to a conversation I had the night before with an old high school friend. When I said I was going to see a critically endangered American chestnut, he more or less asked, "Who gives a shit if some tree goes extinct?" Aware of my leanings, he was gentler than that, but he did press me on why we should spend taxpayer dollars to ward off the extinction of some clearly maladapted, immune-challenged tree. I talked like an ecologist, mentioning the unknown interconnections with other species and how the extinction of the chestnut might trigger the extinctions of other species. I also mentioned the important commodities that could result from the chestnut's resurgence: timber and edible nuts. But I wasn't very convincing with either argument, because even I didn't believe these were good reasons for saving the chestnut or possibly any endangered species.

The reality is that a lot of critically endangered species probably aren't ecologically important to other species—they are already endangered and therefore not numerous enough to have significant ecosystem influence. And saving them because they have monetary value is a risky proposition that potentially leads to monoculture chestnut plantations at the expense of other species without obvious monetary value. In truth, I believe the only real reason for saving the chestnut and other endangered species is because we can save them and it is morally right to do so. I didn't mention this reason to my friend because I know he would have scoffed at a philosophical answer rather than a scientific or economic one, but after spending time with Ron and Murray and the chestnuts, I am more convinced than ever that this is the right answer to an often difficult question.

So I drive with renewed hope for the landscape and more passion for the persistence of its rarest species, even those rare species that seemingly offer no economic or ecological rationale to justify saving them. Now, if only I can carry this good mood home with me. Less snippy with Briana, more energetic with the kids, and less exasperated with my parents. Good intentions always, I think, but we are measured by our actions.

The very next day we head to the Toronto Zoo. I am going to tour their captive breeding facilities, and Briana is going to tour the kids around the African savannah. I am loading the kids into the van when my dad appears carrying the extension ladder.

"What are you doing?"

"The eaves troughs need cleaning," he says.

"Let me clean them tomorrow," I say.

"Don't be silly."

"Don't be crazy."

"You're too busy."

"No," I say. "I'll have lots of time tomorrow."

And with a shake of his head, he climbs up onto the roof and starts scooping guck from the gutters. I sit in the van grinding my teeth, while the kids scream madly at the injustice of their renewed imprisonment. Then Briana appears with a backpack full of diapers, drinks, and snacks.

"What's the matter?" she asks.

I don't reply but instead back out of the driveway with a tire-squealing jolt.

"Everybody wave at Grampa," Briana says, and everyone waves, even Finn, who has just figured out waving. My dad waves back, a jittery off-balance wave that almost sends him somersaulting to the ground below.

We arrive at the zoo three hours before my appointment so that Brora has plenty of time to see the animals that currently comprise 70 percent of her vocabulary... lions and tigers and the linguistically challenging hippopotamus. At the polar bear enclosure, I sneak away for a meeting with Maria Franke, the curator of mammals and person in charge of ferret and marmot captive breeding programs.

Maria and I visit the black-footed ferret facility first. I am lucky because the facility doesn't receive many visitors in order to limit disturbance and prevent disease transmission—I will only get to see the ferrets from behind glass and after suiting up in scrubs. As we enter the facility, we are greeted by one of the ferret handlers and a bank of closed-circuit television sets that display the interior of each ferret cage. Most of the ferrets are offscreen sleeping, but after a few minutes, I see the slender, mink-like silhouette of a ferret as it darts across the screen.

Brora at the Toronto Zoo

We head over to the window that looks into the ferret enclosure. While I watch an incredibly cute ferret dart around its cage, Maria continues to chat away about artificial insemination and hormone monitoring—the zookeeper's vocabulary, I discover, only partially overlaps the wildlife ecologist's vocabulary. "After leaving this facility," Maria says, "all of our ferrets go to a ferret boot camp in Colorado, where they get to hunt prairie dogs and live in real burrows."

I want to ask good questions, but I am completely distracted—I still can't shake the seared image of my off-balance father waving to us from the roof, the driveway below eager to shatter every fragile bone. Plus, there was that conversation with my mother this morning in which she asked me six times within the span of four minutes if we would be home in time for dinner. Her short-term memory loss has increased dramatically since our last visit, a worrying trend that is only going to get worse.

I want to ask Maria why the environment is so artificial, certainly more pet store or sterile lab than Great Plain. I want to ask how any ferret born and raised in this sterile environment can ever really be ready for reintroduction. I want to ask why their cages— wooden boxes connected by dryer tubing—look more suited to pet hamsters than wild ferrets. But I don't. I'm worried she has already answered these questions, but my distracted mind has nodded right through the explanation. Presumably, they are more worried about controlling disease in the breeding colony than naturalizing the environment, which I guess makes some sense, because the ferrets are susceptible to several common diseases, such as canine distemper. And despite my concerns, the zoo is clearly doing things right, because the ferret reintroductions have been pretty successful, though there are still real challenges ahead.

Vancouver Island marmot

We leave the ferret facilities and walk the short distance to the Vancouver Island marmot enclosure. This facility is a little more naturalized—at least there is a fresh breeze blowing through and some natural light. Right away, we see two marmot pups poking their white-tipped noses out of a nest box. Maria is excited—visitors, she says, typically don't get to see ferrets and marmots, because they are usually asleep or hiding. It's more rewarding, I say, to see them in the wild. Sure it is, she says, but without captive breeding, there wouldn't be any left in the wild to see. And, of course, she is absolutely right—captive breeding is a necessary evil, a necessary tool in the conservation biologists' arsenal. It would be much better to intervene when the species in question is still common, to save habitat and prevent exploitation long before drastic measures such as captive breeding are required. But for many species it is already too late for such benign intervention. Although I am somewhat repulsed by the thought of keeping any wild animal in captivity, I am more horrified by extinction.

After the tour, I rendezvous with the family at the elephant enclosure. Briana is sunburned, Finn is asleep, and Brora is a zombie.

"What was your favorite animal?" I ask.

"Tiger poop," Brora says, falling into my arms.

I pick her up and carry her back toward the van. She is asleep before we make it out of the African savannah. We are just strapping everyone into the van when the cell phone rings.

"Are you planning on being home for dinner?" my mom asks.

"No," I say. "We won't be home until about eight."

the ghost
BIRD

"The bird captured on video is clearly
an ivory-billed woodpecker. Amazingly, America
may have another chance to protect
the future of this spectacular bird and the
awesome forests in which it lives."
JOHN FITZPATRICK, director of the Cornell Lab
of Ornithology, statement to the Associated Press

Two days later, we leave my parents' house on the next leg of our road trip. Briana and the kids are somewhat refreshed, I think, but I feel like I spent the entire visit in a constant state of worry. Worried that the kids were too loud, worried that the dog was going to dig up my dad's whole backyard, worried that Briana would finally get fed up with my grumpiness, and, of course, worried about my parents' health.

Yet neither am I relieved to be hitting the road. I am tired of driving, tired of strapping the screaming kids into their car seats, tired of never knowing where we are going to spend the night, tired of motels, and tired of tenting. And yet, here we are, heading south, way south, south of the Mason-Dixon line on the most poorly planned portion of the trip. I might have turned toward home at this point except for Briana, who is becoming more invigorated by the trip the further we get into it. She is relishing the day-to-day challenges, and I am not, at least not for the moment.

Our first endangered species stop is at Point Pelee National Park, the most southern scrap of mainland in Canada. There we are going to make a quick stop to see the federally endangered eastern prickly pear cactus. First, though, we camp for the night at Wheat-

Brora screaming

ley Provincial Park, which at $38 a night is the most expensive campsite of the trip so far by about $13—no wonder we are the only people there.

The campsite is infested with mosquitoes, and the washroom looks like it hasn't been scrubbed hard since it was built in 1973—plus, there are the ticks, ticks, and more ticks. I grew up in this part of Ontario, and I remember having a tick on me perhaps once a year, but now they seem almost as numerous as the mosquitoes. What has changed? Perhaps the pesticides that were keeping them in check are now illegal? Perhaps this is just an extraordinarily ticky year? I don't know, but I don't like it.

Plus, there is a thunderstorm booming ominously over Lake Erie, and the previous night there was a mini-tornado in nearby Leamington. Before having kids, I wouldn't have noticed these risks. Watching a thunderstorm over Lake Erie from a tent would have seemed romantic instead of nerve-wracking.

Anyway, it's not all bad—the surrounding forest is a lovely scrap of Carolinian Canada, and I suspect this is the only place in Canada where you can camp under a solid canopy of hickory trees.

We survive the night. The storm blasted down thirty minutes of heavy rain at one point, but the lightning remained offshore. I make pancakes for breakfast and deliver them to the tent, along with a pretty fine cup of coffee for Briana and me. Then we drive to Point Pelee, which is only ten minutes away.

At the visitor's center, I ask where I might find a patch of eastern prickly pear.

"Follow me," the naturalist says. "There's a patch about two minutes from here."

The two of us walk out to the patch, look at the cacti, and shrug our shoulders—certainly trying to see endangered animals is a lot more challenging and exciting than trying to see endangered plants. The eastern prickly pear (*Opuntia humifusa*) is one of those species that range across North America but only scrape into the very south of Canada. We've seen closely related species of prickly pear all across the continent, so I find it hard to get excited about this rather scrappy patch, which is only of interest from a conservation perspective because it happens to be north of the border.

"How do you know that these are native cacti and not transplanted cacti from god-knows-where?" I ask, knowing that prickly pear transplant easily and are found in gardens everywhere.

"We aren't sure of the exact origins of any individual patch," she says, "but we are confident that there was probably some prickly pear in Ontario prior to European arrival in the region."

"Fair enough," I say, nodding.

"I get more excited about birds," she finally confides.

"Me too," I say.

"A pair of prothonotary warblers is actually nesting in the park this year," she whispers, after ensuring no birders are within earshot. The prothonotary warbler (*Protonotaria citrea*) is a gorgeous warbler, yellow as a lemon, and, like the prickly pear, endangered in Canada but relatively common south of the border. "We haven't had a nesting prothonotary in a few years, so we're all pretty excited."

"Any chance we can check it out?" I ask.

"I can't get away from the desk for that long, but I can tell you where to find it as long as you keep the location to yourself. If word gets out, it could become a bit of a zoo."

"Deal," I say. Then, despite her beckoning desk, we get into a twenty-minute conversation about the recent spring migration—the park is globally famous for the spring migration of birds and the fall migration of monarch butterflies. The naturalist returns to her desk, and I check my watch—I have an hour before I am supposed to rendezvous with the family. Time enough, I think, to find a prothonotary warbler given the detailed directions. I jog down the whispered trail, pausing only to let a gaggle of wild turkeys (*Meleagris gallopavo*) strut across the trail; wild turkeys were in real trouble by the 1970s, because of overhunting and habitat loss, but they have been successfully reintroduced throughout much of their historical range. I slow as I near the described nest location and let my ears guide me—the naturalist described the prothonotary's call as a loud "tweet, tweet, tweet, tweet"—and sure enough, I find the glorious singing male without too much fuss, despite the cacophony of various birdsongs emanating from the forest. Finding an endangered species isn't that hard if you know the specific tree to look in. Through my binoculars, I watch the male flit through the canopy for a few minutes before it disappears deeper into the forest. Then I start jogging back to the trailhead, back to the family.

Before leaving the park, we simply must stand on the tip of Point Pelee, a constantly shifting sand spit that juts well out into Lake Erie. When I was a kid, we used to come here to swim, and I know there are pictures in my parents' crawl space of me standing at the tip of the point. So we walk out to the tip, crossing a marker on the trail that delineates latitude forty-two degrees north, the same latitude as northern California. For a few minutes, we are the most southerly people in mainland Canada. Uninhabited Middle Island, which lies south of inhabited Pelee Island, is the most southerly landmass in Canada. Middle Island was recently purchased by the Nature Conservancy of Canada and then given to Parks Canada.

Pictures on the point acquired, we drive through Essex County along the shore of Lake Erie. I haven't driven this route in twenty years, and it seems largely unchanged, except for the giant wind turbines and solar farms. The Ontario government recently made such ventures profitable by allowing anyone to sell electricity back into the grid, and green energy projects, such as wind and solar, receive a premium per kilowatt-hour. Clearly, the premium was enough incentive to cause a green energy boom here in Essex County, one of the windiest and sunniest areas in Canada. And, by all accounts, the county could use a little financial boom.

En route to my cousin's house for the night, we stop at the Ojibway Prairie Complex in Windsor, Ontario, to take a quick peek at this unique habitat. However, the park interpreters are rude and lazy—too busy stuffing their faces with coffee and donuts and being miserable to discuss the ecological importance of the park and its locally endangered species. Completely disappointed, we leave without even walking a trail. I quietly fume about those useless assholes all the way to Florida.

By 5 PM, we are at my cousin's house for a night of aunts and uncles and kids. My cousin and I go for a drive in the van to pick up the pizza.

"You've gotta be kidding me," he says. "You're driving around the frigging continent without a GPS!"

The next day, we cross back into the U.S. and head south on I75. We slog our way through Detroit, Toledo, Dayton, and Cincinnati before eventually finding a campsite across the Ohio River in Kentucky. A long day on the miserable I75, but our intent after two weeks of relative stasis is to get to Florida relatively quickly.

The private campsite is a little hillbilly-ish—parties around the campfire, pit bulls running around off leash, and shoeless old men in overalls fishing for catfish in the river—but we sleep like the dead until 4 AM, when the rain starts. I drift in and out of sleep, listening to the rain and distant thunder. But then, seemingly out of nowhere, a huge blast of thunder booms directly overhead, followed closely by an intense flash of lightning. The next boom is perhaps the loudest clap of thunder I have ever heard in my life, and growing up in southern Ontario, I have experienced a lot of thunderstorms. The lightning that follows within a few seconds flashes the whole campsite like a massive strobe.

"We need to get in the van fast," I say.

"Okay," Briana says.

"You carry Finn," I say, "and I'll carry Brora."

And with that, we grab the kids and run through the crazy storm to the van.

It's only thirty feet to the van, but we're drenched by the time we slam the doors shut. We sit there, watching the lightning flash all around us. Brora and Finn are both screaming madly, and Adie thinks we are playing a game of some sort— for a very skittish dog, she is remarkably unaffected by the thunder. In the van, I am more relaxed because I know we are at least protected from the lightning, a moderate risk beneath the aluminum tent frame. But I also know that we are in the heart of Tornado Alley, and it has been a very active season— the worst being the Joplin, Missouri, tornado, which killed more than 150 people only a month ago. I turn on the radio and Briana scans for a local weather report, while the rain blasts down and the thunder booms. It takes five minutes to find a weather report: we are under a thunderstorm warning but, thankfully, no tornado warning yet. Finn falls back to sleep in Briana's arms, and then Brora does, too. Another ten minutes pass before the thunderstorm starts to wane—we sit there cradling the sleeping kids and listen to the thunder move off.

We sit in the car until it is light enough for me to pack down the tent, which I do redneck-style, dressed only in my underwear to avoid soaking any more clothes. I throw everything into the rooftop box, pull on my shorts and a T-shirt, and drive us back to the highway through a completely flooded landscape. Overnight, every creek has spilled its banks; each hill is now an island.

In Kentucky, we switch to 165, which is slightly less busy but otherwise indistinguishable from 175. For the first time on the trip since the 15 corridor, I am more worried about cultural extinction than species extinction. I have had moments of concern almost everywhere, but this soulless stretch of busy interstate has me terrified for our culture. Each interstate exit offers up the same blend of Cracker Barrel crap, the same thicket of billboards polluting the sky.

We endure six hours of driving, interrupted by a roadside picnic and a personal meltdown when we spend an hour and a half trying to find a grocery store among all of the IHOPS, Waffle Houses, Shoney's, Shari's, Stuckey's, Sonics, and Carl's Jr.s—in addition to the major fast food chains. It is a truly remarkable blend of trans fats and acrylamide.

How in the hell, we wonder, do people eat in Louisville or Bowling Green?

But all is not lost. We find a lovely campsite at a state park in Tennessee. The warden, a big man who has clearly processed his share of trans fats in his day, has a perfect southern drawl. I exchange repeated pleasantries with him just so that I can listen to him chew his vowels a little longer.

"I done heard we're fixin' for a big storm," he says. "Y'all take shelter in the comfort station if it gets bad."

The next day, we roll into Alabama, which is a little terrifying in a *Deliverance* kind of way. At least Tennessee has an NHL team. And suddenly it is hot again, Alabama hot, ninety-five degrees Fahrenheit and humid. At a rest area, Brora makes me jealous when she gets to play under a water faucet completely naked for an hour.

We splurge on a motel with a pool. It is Brora's second birth-day—swimming and cake are her only requests—and although we already had a party for her at my parents' house, we can't let the actual day pass unnoticed.

Finally, we get off the main highways and zigzag across southern rural Alabama. Our destination is the Choctawhatchee River in the Florida Panhandle, where ivory-billed woodpeckers have recently been seen and heard on numerous occasions. If true, these sightings, along with similar recent sightings in Arkansas, are really remarkable, because the ivory-billed woodpecker was thought to have been extinct since the 1940s.

The ivory-billed woodpecker (*Campephilus principalis*), with a thirty-inch wingspan, was the biggest woodpecker in North America and one of the biggest woodpeckers in the world. It roamed the southern forests of the United States, from the cypress swamps of Florida to the pine forests of Texas. As long as those old-growth forests were intact, the ivory-billed woodpecker persisted at low densities across the landscape. However, most of these southern forests were cleared by the early 1900s, and by the 1920s, the species was in real trouble. As goes the habitat, so goes the species—the last confirmed sighting of an ivory-billed was in the soon-to-be-logged Singer Tract in Louisiana in 1944.

Over the next sixty years, there were occasional ivory-billed sightings across its historical range, but none were officially verified. Most were easily dismissed as the fanciful musings of amateur bird watchers, but a few of the sightings were a little more credible. Then, in 2005, everything changed—at least momentarily—when the Cornell Lab of Ornithology published an article in the journal *Science* that confirmed the presence of an ivory-billed woodpecker in Arkansas's Big Woods. I remember hearing a brief news bulletin on the radio and being immediately skeptical, but then I read online that the claim was being made by Cornell in *Science*, and my skepticism was replaced by amazement.

Holy shit, I thought, somehow, a handful survived.

My amazement was short-lived. Within days, other experts had analyzed the "data," which consisted primarily of a very grainy video, and raised concerns about the veracity of the conclusions. For example, one rebuttal in *The Auk* harshly stated that "for scientists to label sight reports and questionable photographs as 'proof' of such an extraordinary record is delving into 'faith-based' ornithology and doing a disservice to science."

The problem was that the video did not clearly differentiate the supposed ivory-billed woodpecker from the ubiquitous pileated woodpecker. On quick glance, the pileated woodpecker is similar in appearance to the ivory-billed, though the pileated is slightly smaller, has a different plumage pattern on its wings, and has a darker bill. None of these differences are clearly denoted in the video. Within a few weeks, I was back to being skeptical, albeit a little more hopeful that more robust data would soon be collected. That data, however, never materialized, despite intensive searches spanning five years.

Shortly after the Arkansas "discovery," another research group, from Auburn University in Alabama and the University of Windsor in Ontario, claimed the ivory-billed woodpecker also persisted along the Choctawhatchee River in Florida's Panhandle. The data in this case consisted of nonphotographed sightings and numerous sound recordings. However, as in Arkansas, five more years of intensive searching did not yield any truly conclusive data—good photos, feathers, DNA, or a specimen.

Eventually, almost everyone returned to their pre-2005 position—the ivory-billed is unfortunately extinct and probably has been since the 1940s. Even the Auburn/Windsor team eventually concluded on their blog that "either the excitement of the ivorybill hunt causes competent birders to see and hear things that do not exist and leads competent sound analysts to misidentify hundreds of recorded sounds, or the few ivorybills in the Choctawhatchee River Basin are among the most elusive birds on the planet." I doubt that one of the largest woodpeckers in the world could really be that elusive, but I don't doubt that fine birders, like all of us, can be influenced by hope and desire.

But I still want to try to see an ivory-billed woodpecker. At the very least, I want to spend a little time in historic ivory-billed habitat and contemplate the recent controversy. And this is how we find ourselves exploring places along the Choctawhatchee River such as Dead River Road and then heading down a gravel road to a place called Tilley Landing, which was reputed to be one of the locations where ivory-billed woodpeckers were sighted in 2006.

The road to Tilley Landing terminates at a little boat launch in the middle of a mature forest dominated by wide-buttressed cypress trees. The forest looks to be ideal for ivory-billed woodpeckers, which preferred old-growth hardwood swamps with lots of dead and dying trees. We walk down to the water, a swampy little offshoot of the muddy Choctawhatchee, and immediately flush a tricolored heron, a new species for me. As Brora scampers along the shoreline, I follow her closely, thinking it looks like a good spot for an alligator or two. The forest is eerily quiet—no birds singing and, surprisingly, no mosquitoes.

We continue bushwhacking along the shoreline, looking for signs of ivory-bills—peeled bark and/or nest cavities drilled into dead trees about thirty to forty feet above the ground. On a long-dead tree that has toppled partly into the water, a bunch of drilled cavities makes me pause—could these have been drilled by an ivory-billed years ago?

"Imagine if we actually saw one and got a good photo," I say to Briana wistfully. "We'd be famous."

"That's exactly the kind of thinking," she says, "that causes people to see things that don't exist."

Not wanting to get lost in this foreign landscape, we don't wander very far down the river. We return to the parking lot, drag the cooler down to the river, and make a lunch of cheese sandwiches and fresh Alabama watermelon. I eat my sandwich while guarding Brora down by the river.

Then my heart skips a beat—there is a big woodpecker in the trees across the river. Forgetting Brora and the alligators, I fumble for my binoculars and try desperately to get the woodpecker in view, but the bird remains stubbornly fixed to the backside of a big trunk. I wave madly at Briana, mouthing "Bring the camera," which is on our picnic blanket. Briana runs over with Finn asleep in the Man Uterus.

Before I can even tell her where to look, the woodpecker flies out of the forest and diagonally across the river. Thankfully, I brushed up on my field marks last night—the trailing edges of the wings are solid black, making it a pileated woodpecker. No question about it.

ELEVEN

the siren's
SONG

"It was this motley band of modest
peeps and plovers on the beach who reminded me
of the human beings I loved best—the
ones who didn't fit in."
JONATHAN FRANZEN, *The Discomfort Zone:*
A Personal History

After enduring the long drive to Florida, we take a break at
St. Joseph Peninsula State Park, where we spend three nights
camped right on the Gulf of Mexico. The campsites are packed
a little tight, but the beach is awesome. The gulf is like a giant
hot tub, ninety degrees Fahrenheit at least, and as calm as a
birdbath. Surprisingly, there is no sign of any oil from the massive BP oil spill in 2010. We spend three days neck-deep in the
soup, teaching Brora to swim.

Then we spend three nights sweating to death in the tent.
Camping next to us is a four-hundred-pound biker dude and I
have no idea how he survives the sultry nights. The gulf is so

warm that there is really no cooling effect at nighttime. The days are ninety-five degrees Fahrenheit and humid, and the nights are eighty-five degrees Fahrenheit and humid, which turns the tent into a Crock-Pot of sorts. Poor little Finn suffers the worst—by day three he has developed a worrying heat rash.

The next species on our list is the red-cockaded woodpecker (*Picoides borealis*). We leave St. Joseph Peninsula as early as we can manage, 9 AM, and drive along the gulf until we cut north on State Road 65. This road cuts through the western portion of Apalachicola National Forest, which supposedly has a healthy population of red-cockaded woodpeckers.

More typical of the woodpecker family than the massive ivory-billed woodpecker, the red-cockaded woodpecker is a little smaller than an American robin. The plumage is primarily black and white, though the male does have a little red stripe, not usually visible, behind its eye, called a cockade. Its back is barred, and it has bright white cheeks and a black cap. These birds live in cooperative breeding groups, with young from one year typically helping to raise the subsequent generation. Ecologically, red-cockaded woodpeckers perform the important service of an ecosystem engineer by excavating cavities that are eventually used by many other species of birds and other animals.

The story of the red-cockaded woodpecker parallels that of the ivory-billed woodpecker, though it does not end on such a tragic note. Red-cockaded woodpeckers, like ivory-billed woodpeckers, were dependent on mature southern forests, particularly longleaf pine forests. As these forests disappeared, so did the woodpeckers. Thankfully, perhaps in part because of the earlier demise of the ivory-billed, there was the necessary political will to reverse the decline of the red-cockaded woodpecker. By the 1980s, several groups were preserving and managing habitat around known nest sites. Today, there are an estimated twelve thousand birds, which sounds like quite a few, though this still only constitutes a very small percentage, perhaps 1 percent, of the historical population size. Consequently, the species is still considered to be vulnerable to extinction.

Trying to find a common species on any particular day can be a challenge, even if you're in an ecosystem that you are familiar with. Trying to find a rare species in an ecosystem you have never set foot in is obviously way more difficult. Thankfully, when it comes to red-cockaded woodpeckers, I have a few tactical advantages: I know they are common along this stretch of road, I know that trees with active cavities glisten from all the sap being released from recent cavity excavations, and I know that local biologists spray-paint white rings around trees with active cavities.

I've got a chance, I think, as we drive north into the pine forests of Apalachicola.

We are perhaps thirty minutes down the road when we see our first trees ringed with paint, but the paint looks old and I wonder if these trees still contain active cavities. We decide to head a little farther north, to an area referred to as "Wilma," where a local birder suggested via email that we would be certain to see one. There we start to see more trees ringed with paint, a few of which are quite whitish with fresh sap.

Briana pulls way over onto the shoulder—there have been a few wobbly logging trucks on the road but no one else—and I get out with binoculars and tripod/camera. The air is oppressively hot, almost overwhelming, especially after a couple of hours in the air-conditioned van. We hate AC under normal Canadian conditions, but the Deep South has forced us to adapt, particularly with Finn all covered in a pimply heat rash.

I walk slowly toward one of the longleaf pine trees ringed in white. This forest was logged heavily in the late 1800s and then logged again during World War II. Commercial logging continues to this day, though regulations are in place to protect the habitat of the red-cockaded woodpecker. The third-growth forest makes for easy walking, because the trees are widely spaced and the undergrowth, mainly saw palmetto of some sort, is minimal. It is a stark contrast to the thick cypress swamp along the Choctawhatchee.

When I am about sixty-five feet from the tree, I hopefully set up my tripod and position my camera for a picture. Within my field of view, I can see four ringed trees, so I figure this must be the center of one group's home range. All I have to do now is wait. And wait. And wait.

Then, finally, I hear a number of birds, probably woodpeckers, chattering across the road from my location. I race over and, sure enough, there are some woodpeckers moving through the forest. I quietly pursue them and, eventually, I get a quick look. Red-cockaded woodpeckers for sure, three or four of them. I set up the tripod and wait for them to move into the open, but they are a rather uncooperative bunch. I manage a few crappy photos before they move farther down the road. I quietly pursue them again, set up the tripod, and hope they will move closer. They don't—instead they cross the road and disappear farther into the forest.

I trot back to the van a sweaty, disgusting mess. I have been gone almost two hours, which is an hour and fifty-five minutes longer than I said I would be. But the ever-accommodating Briana is unfazed—she and Brora are strolling along the bubbling asphalt, and Finn is asleep in his car seat.

"Sorry," I say, "I was in hot pursuit."

"I saw you run across the road twice," Briana says, "so I figured you were after your woodpecker."

We jump in the van, blast the AC, and continue down the road to the nearby campsite.

When we pull into the empty campground, the dashboard thermometer, which is perhaps the best piece of dashboard technology since the invention of the radio, indicates a whopping one hundred degrees Fahrenheit. We are scared to turn off the AC and open the doors.

I ask the obvious—"Can we do this?"

"We're already here," says Briana.

So we set up the tent. Eat some fruit. Drink some water. Then I fill the tub for the kids to play in—a tub of water will occupy Brora for hours. Briana and I sit like cadavers in our lawn chairs until sunset.

That night, I don't sleep a wink. Instead, I lie spread-eagle in my sad underwear, fanning myself and Finn with Briana's terribly out-of-place *Bon Appétit* magazine. The not sleeping makes it easy to get up at 5 AM to try to get a better photo of the woodpecker.

I return to the same forest patch and find the same wary group quickly enough, but they never come within good photo range. I take a hundred very long-range shots, every one terrible. Frustrated, I return to the campsite at 8:30 AM.

"Let's get the hell out of here," Briana says, holding up a sweaty, naked Finn, who is now officially one big heat rash.

We leave the national forest and drive a circuitous route
around Tallahassee. Several times, we are blasted with crazy,
mad thunderstorms. At one point, a storm erupts and we watch
the temperature drop from ninety-seven degrees Fahrenheit to
a blessed seventy-two degrees in a matter of minutes. By 5 PM,
the post-storm temperature remains below eighty-five degrees,
so we decide to camp again. This time we camp at Manatee
Springs State Park in hopes of seeing … a manatee.

West Indian manatees (*Trichechus manatus*) are fully aquatic
marine mammals that look slightly hippo-like. Take a hippo
and replace the front legs with flippers and the back legs with
one mermaid-like flipper. Then replace the head with a walrus-
like head, minus the tusks. Wait—maybe the walrus is a better
likeness. Take a walrus and remove the tusks and then transport it from the Arctic Ocean to a Florida swamp and, voila,
you've got a manatee. You get the idea anyway—a big, awkward-
looking, yet surprisingly gentle herbivore that seems quite out
of place in this era and ecosystem.

The West Indian manatee is one of three species of manatee,
the other two being the Amazonian manatee and the West African manatee. The three species of manatee are grouped with
the similar-looking dugong of the Indo-Pacific region in the
mammalian order Sirenia, and all four species are vulnerable
to extinction. Sirenia also included the now-extinct Steller's sea
cow, which was by far the largest member of the order and found
throughout the North Pacific. The sea cow was first described
scientifically by naturalist Georg Steller in 1741, by which time
it was already greatly reduced in number—and within twenty-
seven years of this description, it was hunted to extinction.
The order gets its name from the mermaid-like sirens of Greek

mythology, who would reportedly seduce sailors into ship-wrecking upon their island, though you would have to be truly lovesick to be seduced by a manatee. DNA evidence suggests the closest living relative of the manatees are the elephants, though the two groups probably split more than 50 million years ago.

The Florida manatees (*Trichechus manatus latirostris*) are actually a subspecies of West Indian manatees. They are the largest subspecies and have the northernmost range of any manatee. Like all manatees, they are largely herbivorous, feeding on a wide assortment of sea grasses and such, and like a lot of endangered species, they have a relatively low reproductive rate—females typically have one calf every three years. In winter, they concentrate around freshwater springs in Florida, such as Manatee Springs, that have a constant water temperature year round. However, in summer, when warm water is everywhere, they disperse along the coasts of the Gulf of Mexico and the Atlantic. In the summer of 2006, one manatee actually wandered as far north as New York City. These summer wanderings add substantially to our difficulty in spotting them—in winter months manatee sightings are practically guaranteed at Manatee Springs, but a summer sighting is quite unlikely. Florida manatee numbers have rebounded modestly over the past decade, and there are probably now well over three thousand individuals. Currently listed as "endangered" in the United States, there has been much discussion as to whether the manatee should be downlisted to "threatened" as a result of this rebound.

We set up our camp, eat a quick dinner, and then stroll down to the spring. A natural spring is a spot where a groundwater aquifer naturally flows to the surface. Springs are classified by the amount of water they discharge, and Manatee Springs is a big one, discharging an average of 100 million gallons of water per day. This substantial discharge immediately creates a small river, which flows for perhaps 1,600 feet before discharging into the large Suwannee River. The temperature of the water emanating from the spring is seventy-two degrees Fahrenheit year round, making it the warmest water around during the winter months. The manatees congregate at the spring in winter to take advantage of this relatively warm water to calve and simply hang around.

The spring is visually strik-
ing. Aquamarine water surges
out of the ground before flowing
through a thick forest of moss-
covered cypress trees. Brora and I
step into the water up to our knees.
Even at seventy-two degrees Fahrenheit, the water feels icy cold on
this muggy evening. Then we walk
the boardwalk that parallels the
entire length of the spring's run

Manatee Springs

out to the Suwannee River. At the river, we hang out on a dock and watch some big fish jump. No manatees and no alligators, but the sunset illuminates a massive wall of thunderclouds and eventually turns them as pink as salmon roe.

We return to the campsite and crawl into the tent. I am exhausted because I haven't slept well in five nights as a result of the extreme heat. But tonight, the air temperature is a relatively cool eighty degrees Fahrenheit and dropping. As soon as it's dark, however, the tree frogs start calling in the thousands, a massive trilling horde of American green tree frogs. Then a barred owl starts calling from the tree above the tent. A rival soon takes up the challenge and adds to the chorus. The two owls duel back and forth for an hour. I hadn't realized that barred owls ranged all the way down to Florida. I had thought of them as predominantly Canadian owls that were expanding south into the western United States. But, in the east, they range down to the very tip of Florida and live in a great variety of habitats—it is exactly this remarkable adaptability that will make it difficult for spotted owls to successfully compete with them along the West Coast.

The combination of trilling frogs and hooting owls is acoustically overwhelming—so loud that we have to shout to each other to be heard above the great hullabaloo of natural selection. Despite the cacophony, or perhaps because of it, all five of us spend the night in deep hibernation.

In the morning, Adie and I walk down to the spring and out to the dock for sunrise. We don't see any manatees, but we do see a few early morning fishermen bombing down the river in their bass boats. Although habitat loss is the most serious long-term threat to the Florida manatees, the greatest human-related threat to manatees in the short term is collisions with watercraft. Almost a hundred manatees were confirmed to have been killed by watercraft in 2010, a significant number for a population numbering only a few thousand individuals. Manatees can be crushed by hulls or sliced open by propellers, injuries that are not necessarily immediately fatal but can result in a lethal infection.

I return to the campsite modestly depressed by the lack of manatees in Manatee Springs, but I'm not worried about missing a manatee altogether, since there are several manatee-watching companies that guarantee manatee sightings during the winter and summer. Most of these companies also offer the rather horrifying option of allowing you to "swim with the manatees," if that somehow floats your boat.

Later that morning, after oatmeal and coffee and a little birding from the picnic table, we suit up for a swim in the spring. Swimming is prohibited in the winter, when the habitat is critical for the manatees, but in the summer it's a legitimate swimming hole. The water is so cold that I have to force myself to go in above my crotch, but Brora could play in it all day. Finally, when Brora has turned a good Scottish blue, we decide to rent a canoe for an hour or two of paddling "way down upon de Swanee Ribber," which Stephen Foster immortalized in his song "Old Folks at Home." The river gets its start in the Okefenokee Swamp and flows 247 miles to the Gulf of Mexico.

Briana and I have never canoed together, and neither of us has paddled with a toddler, an infant, and a dog, so there is a lot to negotiate at the start. Eventually, we decide that I will paddle and she will manage the unruly passengers. I spent multiple summers working from a canoe, but I rarely paddle in my current life, which for me is a significant cost of my urban existence. Two minutes on the water is all it takes for my muscles to remember the strokes and the rhythm, and then we are off, down the spring's run and out in the wide, slow Suwannee.

"I'll kill you if we tip," Briana says, clutching little Finn like they're on the deck of the sinking *Titanic.*

"Have no fear," I sing in a manly tone—the canoe is big and girthy, a real family boat that would be hard to tip, but I stay near the shoreline regardless.

"In his life jacket," Briana says, "Finn will bob around like alligator bait ... what the heck is that?"

"What?"

"That," Briana says, pointing out into the river, "is a manatee."

The manatee is swimming right toward us.

"Get the camera!" I shout.

"It's in the backpack behind you!" Briana shouts.

I fumble to get the camera out and then check the setting, which is still set for nighttime photography around the campsite. But there's no real rush because the manatee is setting a gentle pace, the exact opposite of our Yellowstone wolf. Eventually, I start rattling off shots, a hundred when three or four would do—I have no idea how best to take a shot into water.

West Indian manatee

I stand to improve the camera angle and the big boat wobbles from the sudden movement. Then we watch as the manatee swims right past us, perhaps twenty or thirty feet off our starboard. The manatee is, I imagine, small for a manatee, maybe seven feet long, and more slender and agile than I would have thought from the photographs and videos I have seen. Much to my surprise, it does look almost mermaid-like as it glides past us, seductive and serene.

TWELVE

alligator
ALLEY

Buttercup: "That's the fire swamp!
We'll never survive."
Westley: "Nonsense! You're only saying that
because no one ever has."
WILLIAM GOLDMAN, *The Princess Bride*

On a whim, we rent a tiny beach bungalow south of Clearwater for five days of classic Florida vacationing. We swim in the overheated gulf; we build a hundred sandcastles; we sleep in air-conditioned comfort. For a treat on the Fourth of July, we barbecue a chunk of red grouper and some vegetables for dinner and then eat a tub of ice cream on the beach with fireworks exploding all around us.

"Out of curiosity," Briana asks me under the rocket's red glare, "how sustainable is red grouper anyway?"

"The salesperson was more sommelier than fishmonger," I say. "She recommended a Riesling to accompany the grouper."

Back in the bungalow, Briana fires up the computer and does a quick Google search.

"The red grouper," she announces, "is listed as 'near threatened' by the International Union for the Conservation of Nature. That makes it more endangered than the burrowing owl and swift fox."

"Great," I say. "We might as well have eaten a piping plover. Thank God it was delicious."

"I don't think," Briana says, "we should let our yuppie taste buds justify the ecological atrocity."

"Agreed," I say.

In truth, I am not at all surprised by the near-threatened status of the red grouper (*Epinephelus morio*). The gourmet fish-and-wine store where I bought it only had three species of fresh fish available—red grouper, black grouper, and yellowedge grouper—all of which turned out to be species at risk. This endangered selection is pretty typical of most fish stores or the fish counter at your grocery store. If you want to see three endangered species in one day, the easiest way to do it is to visit your local fishmonger and browse the selection. And even if the species you chose for dinner isn't yet a species of concern, just wait a few years and it probably will be—commercial fishing is remarkably efficient at turning even a superabundant species into an endangered species via intense exploitation. The Atlantic cod is but one example, albeit the best, of a species that went from being one of the most numerous vertebrates on the planet to global endangerment, and the sole culprit for this dramatic change in abundance was commercial fishing.

In addition to overfishing, there is also the very real possibility that the fish you chose for dinner isn't the fish you thought it was—eco-fraud is rampant within the fishing industry and takes a wide variety of forms. For example, a species of lesser value can be substituted for a higher-value species—you might think you are eating red grouper, but in reality you are eating mercury-rich tilefish. Or you think you are eating a fish harvested in a sustainable manner—pole-caught tuna, for example—but in reality you are eating tuna caught in a drift net. Or perhaps you think you are eating a sockeye salmon fished from a river with a healthy population, but you are actually eating sockeye salmon destined for a different river. The fraud can happen on the boat, at the processing plant, through a middleman, or in the restaurant. Such fish fraud is difficult to police and often requires DNA analysis. Plus, governments have been universally negligent with their policing efforts. A recent investigative report by the *Boston Globe*—just one of many similar reports—found that of 148 samples of fish taken from restaurants, grocery stores, and fish stores, a whopping 48 percent were mislabeled as a more expensive or more sustainable type of fish. For example, the "Key West grouper" at T.G.I. Friday's was actually Vietnamese catfish.

For quite a while now (really, ever since working for a winter as an at-sea observer on bottom trawlers fifteen years ago), I have been of the opinion that wild-caught fish are perhaps the least sustainable food choice one could make. The data on the impact of commercial fishing on fish stocks and the broader environment are irrefutable. One factor contributing to the problem is the rather weak data suggesting that fish are an important part of a healthy diet—in fact, we are often told by our doctors to eat fish two or three times a week for optimal health. However, the already overtaxed fisheries cannot tolerate such levels of consumption, particularly now that there are 7 billion of us on the planet, all of us equally entitled to a healthy diet.

Voluntary avoidance of certain fish species by savvy consumers, as advocated by several well-meaning groups like Sea Watch, won't solve the problems with the global fishery. In fact, the "good to eat" may actually encourage more eco-fraud. The solution lies in courageous government regulation. Bottom trawlers, for instance, could and should simply be outlawed. I believe that the hope long term, for those of us who want to eat fish, is in aquaculture, though that industry still has a long way to go to achieve sustainability. For example, many farmed fish are now "best choices" according to Sea Watch, but those fish typically eat fish food made from feeder fish such as anchovies—they are simply a commercial fishery once removed. Fish raised on vegetable protein would be a much more sustainable option.

In all of North America, Florida is ecologically unique, a swampy subtropical offshoot. Because of this uniqueness, the state is home to a number of species of birds unique to North America, a few of which are also species of concern. In addition to the red-cockaded woodpecker, three of the most endangered birds in Florida are the Florida scrub jay, the snail kite, and the wood stork. Our goal is to see each of these species en route to the Everglades, home of the elusive Florida panther. We know the panther will be almost impossible to find, so the excursion is really more about seeing the Everglades than seeing the panther itself.

The Florida scrub jay (*Aphelocoma coerulescens*) is the first species we pursue, and it is the only species of bird endemic to Florida, meaning that it is found in Florida and nowhere else. (The red-cockaded woodpecker, in contrast, is found in Florida and numerous other states.) It is a relative of the western scrub jay, the scrub jay that I saw with Adie on the second day of our trip, over two months ago. True to its name, the Florida scrub jay lives in the Florida scrub, an endangered habitat found on sandy ridges in central Florida. Typically, these ridges are sparsely covered in shrubs and oak trees and, historically, wildfires were quite common. The scrubland is easy to convert to subdivisions and agricultural land—at least, easier to convert than Florida swampland—and Florida has seen a great deal of development over the past few decades. Fire suppression is also a threat, because without intermittent forest fires, the scrub habitat is replaced by mature forest, which is less suitable for the scrub jays. Appropriate habitat can be maintained with controlled burns—intentionally set fires that burn back maturing forest and produce the scrubby habitat the scrub jays prefer. Managing disturbances such as fire, rather than preventing them, has become an increasingly important aspect of conservation biology. In 1987, the scrub jay was listed as vulnerable by the Fish and Wildlife Service. Today, the scrub jay is still in trouble and probably still in decline: the best estimate of current population size is perhaps four thousand pairs.

We bid farewell to our beachside bungalow and drive south on I75 to Oscar Scherer State Park, reportedly one of the best spots to see scrub jays. After setting up our tent and eating lunch, we go for a walk on the trail the park naturalist recommends. In the heat, we stagger around the three-mile trail like zombies—midday in the summer is the time for neither birding nor strolling in Florida. We manage to see a couple of blue jays, but no scrub jays.

We return to the campsite, which is partially shaded, and drink gallons of juice and water. Then we go for a swim in the little man-made lake. The water feels cool but only in contrast to the extreme heat of the day, ninety-five degrees Fahrenheit, and the humidity. Florida in July has been more overwhelming temperaturewise than I found India to be, though I have not visited India in the middle of summer.

We are walking back to the campsite when I think I hear a scrub jay calling in the distance (I've obviously never heard a Florida scrub jay in person, but I listened to one online the previous night). Then, sure enough, Briana spies a scrub jay in the top of a tree across the parking lot. As we walk toward the squawking scrub jay, we see two more scrub jays foraging around a picnic table. The two on the ground take flight as we approach, perhaps because Adie is on a long leash. I reel Adie in, and we stand around and watch as the sentinel continues to shout at us.

"Let's get the camera," I say after a few minutes.

We trot to the campsite as quickly as the heat allows and retrieve the camera from the locked van. Then, each carrying a kid, we trot back to the parking lot at double time. Although we were only gone for ten minutes or so, the scrub jays are nowhere to be found. We walk around for an hour trying to find them again, but no luck. Finally, exhausted from the heat, we sit at the picnic table where we first saw the scrub jays. Thinking about how best to reacquire the jays, I consult Briana on our next move.

"What should we do?" I ask.

"Get out of here and find somewhere cooler for Finny," she says, tearing up.

It is the first time on the whole trip she has asked for any change to my imposed itinerary, and I get it—for once, I don't negotiate. We walk back to the campsite, load the kids into the van, and blast the AC at them. I crush the tent into a ball and throw it into the trunk. Then we drive to the air-conditioned comfort of the pet-friendly La Quinta in Naples.

Naples is a wealthy enclave built on the western edge of the Everglades. However, given the sad state of Florida's economy, I am quite certain the swamp will exact its revenge soon enough and reclaim the lost territory. But for now, Naples is a bastion of good coffee and organic groceries, just the elixirs needed to help us reenergize.

American alligator

We take the morning to relax, and by afternoon, we are ready to take a preliminary jaunt into the great swamp. We leave Naples on Route 41, which beelines through the Everglades all the way to Miami. Approximately twenty miles east of Naples, we decide to turn onto Turner River Road, or County Road 839, a rough gravel road that heads north into Big Cypress National Preserve, one of several preserves that protect a big chunk of the Everglades.

Even though it is the dry summer season, the surrounding landscape still seems to be more water than land. And the water is chock-full of alligators. We get out of the van to inspect one pond and count six alligators within fifty feet of us. Even more disconcerting, three of the alligators start swimming leisurely toward us, coming right up to our feet, though our feet have wisely backed away by the time the alligators arrive.

"Someone has been feeding these gators," I say to Briana as I plop Brora up on my shoulders.

We are as far away from British Columbia as we will get on this trip, and at this moment, standing in the oppressively hot swamp with the mosquitoes and alligators circling close, we feel very far away indeed.

Back on Road 839, we creep north at a snake's pace, hoping for a one-in-a-million panther encounter. But the first stretch is all alligators and black vultures. Wherever there is a food source, the black vultures gather in great number to feast. I get out of the car to determine what has attracted one particular group, hoping it isn't a body courtesy of the Miami mafia, but

Black vultures

it is a long-dead alligator that was probably hit by a vehicle or bullet. The black vultures barely move off the carcass as I approach. Have you, I want to ask, seen a panther lately?

The Florida panther (*Puma concolor*) is the same species as the cougar, mountain lion, and puma. The plethora of common names stems from the fact that the species has such a large geographic range, throughout the Americas from Alaska to Argentina. Historically, the cougar ranged almost everywhere in North America, but agricultural development and direct persecution eventually led to the extirpation of the species everywhere east of the Mississippi, except, that is, for the small population that still makes its home in the Everglades. This recently isolated population, which typically numbers fewer than a hundred individuals, has been on the brink of extinction for at least fifty years.

The Florida panther used to be considered a unique subspecies of cougar, but genetic analysis indicated that the Florida population and other North American cougars were genetically very similar. As a result of this genetic similarity—which stems from the fact that the Florida panther was only recently isolated—all North American cougars were eventually amalgamated into a single subspecies. Whereas the Florida scrub jay shared a common ancestor with the western scrub jay many tens of thousands of years ago, the Florida panther shared a common ancestor with other North American cougars only a few hundred years ago. Before development and persecution, Florida panthers would have regularly moved between and swapped genes with adjacent populations, and this gene flow resulted in the genetic uniformity of the various cougar populations. For a wide-ranging species like the cougar, the gene pool was, in fact, the whole continent.

The change in taxonomic status, from unique subspecies to just another population of cougars, has had serious conservation implications; if the Florida panther really is not a genetically unique subspecies, how much effort should be expended trying to ensure its long-term persistence? For instance, the International Union for Conservation of Nature formerly listed the Florida panther as critically endangered, but it was recently dropped from their list entirely. However, it is a mistake to think of the Florida panther as ecologically less important simply because it is not genetically unique; like the wolves of Yellowstone, Florida panthers are important apex predators that will help to maintain ecosystem integrity.

The genetic similarity between the Florida panther and other cougars proved useful when the Florida population seemed destined for extinction in the 1990s. At that time, the population was estimated to be composed of only twenty-six individuals and was therefore considered to be a genetically compromised population. The small population was losing whatever genetic diversity remained, and substantial inbreeding increased the expression of genetic disorders. The population was clearly in an extinction vortex, the downward spiral of a genetically compromised population that ends in extinction. The population decreased not because of faulty genetics but because of habitat loss and overharvesting. But then, after being small for many generations, the population became genetically compromised. Even with habitat secured, the population's compromised genetics prevented a recovery and seemingly guaranteed extinction.

If the Florida panther were a unique species, conservation biologists would have been forced to work with the damaged gene pool as it was, coddling the species back toward health as has been done with the black-footed ferret and California condor. However, with the Florida panther there was another option—translocating some cougars from another location into the Everglades in hopes that an injection of new individuals, and thus new DNA into the gene pool, would increase the vigor of the population. In 1995, eight female cougars from Texas, currently the nearest healthy population, were released into the Everglades, and this genetic enhancement proved successful. The population climbed quickly to around a hundred individuals, which is certainly better than twenty-six, though still not large enough to prevent the population from getting sucked back into the extinction vortex. More translocations will likely be needed in the future if the panther is going to stalk the Everglades indefinitely.

We drive slowly north on Road 839 for two hours until it dead-ends at a deserted campsite. We haven't seen a single vehicle on the road since leaving Route 41, and a lack of cell phone service makes this perhaps the worst place on the whole trip for a vehicle malfunction. But the van is unfazed by the extreme heat, the terrible washboard road, and the inch-thick coating of dust and mosquitoes on the grill.

We slowly head back to Naples, getting out occasionally to take a picture of an alligator and stretch our legs but always being forced back into the van by the heat and hungry mosquitoes, which are more voracious than any Canadian mosquito I've ever encountered. Finally, we arrive in Naples in time for a quick swim and a late dinner.

The next morning, I head out on my own in the predawn to explore the Florida Panther National Wildlife Refuge, which at any given moment might contain ten panthers or so, though each individual would also make use of adjacent parks and private land. The refuge is large, about twenty-six thousand acres, but almost all of it is off limits to the public, except for two short hiking trails. Under the authority of the Endangered Species Act, the refuge was created in 1989, when the panther was on the brink of extinction. In Canada, conservation biologists have always been envious of the strong endangered species legislation in the United States; our Species at Risk Act was enacted much later and is weaker, particularly in its ability to secure necessary habitat.

I arrive at the refuge just as the unforgiving sun is cresting the hazy horizon. Even the long trail is only about a mile and a half long, so I walk slowly and concentrate on watching and listening. Right away, I am rewarded with a good view of a swallow-tailed kite circling overhead, yet another new species for me. Then I see a red-bellied woodpecker—a species I would see on rare occasions flitting from pine to pine when I lived in southern Ontario. At the far end of the trail, I sit quietly with my back to a tree and hope for a panther or even a bear, which is a species of concern in Florida. But it is hard to sit still for long given the damn mosquitoes, which eventually send me running back to the van, back to the family.

We spend the rest of that day at the beach. The following day we explore the north side of Everglades National Park. We don't see a panther, but then again, we weren't expecting to. After searching a hundred wetlands with our binoculars, however, we finally manage to find and photograph a wood stork (*Mycteria americana*) in a roadside ditch. The snail kite (*Rostrhamus sociabilis*) has been less cooperative. I've seen two hawks at a distance that might have been snail kites—they were flying like snail kites—but they never came within close enough range to allow me to get a good look at their field marks.

Both the wood stork and snail kite are endangered in the United States, though both are globally common. They share similar hemispheric ranges, ranging throughout the Amazon watershed and portions of Central America and only clipping the extreme southeastern portion of the United States. The snail kite is confined to southern Florida, whereas the wood stork also ranges into Georgia and South Carolina. Both species are intimately associated with swamps, and Florida has the vast swamps necessary to give both species a toehold in North America.

The wood stork is the only stork native to North America. It is unmistakable—a big white-and-black wading bird with a bald head reminiscent of the head of a California condor. It has a massive beak, much like the long-beaked masks worn at costume parties. It nests in colonies in swamp trees, typically cypress and mangrove, and forages in the swamps for fish and frogs and other morsels by pushing its impressive beak through the muddy water until it detects a prey item and snaps its beak closed. The wood stork is endangered in the United States as a result of habitat loss, especially the draining of swamps. Historically, DDT and other toxins also interfered with its reproductive success.

Wood stork

The snail kite is so named because it eats snails, seemingly odd prey for a hawk. In particular, the snail kite eats tangerine-sized apple snails, and its geographic distribution is tied to the distribution of the apple snail. Drainage of Florida wetlands to make room for ever more agriculture decreased the number and distribution of the snails and thus the populations of snail kites in the United States. The snail kite feeds by flying low and slowly over a swamp and visually searching for a snail to grab with its talons. The snail kite extracts the snail from its shell with its specialized beak—long, slender, and strongly curved. The beak is the snail kite's most distinguishing feature, and it is the feature I failed to see on the two birds I thought might have been snail kites. The coloration and flying pattern seemed right, but the birds were too far away to confirm their identity, given that I only know the species from photographs and YouTube videos.

Finally, after three days in the Everglades and two full weeks in Florida, we turn north for our drive up the Eastern Seaboard. We start by zigzagging across Florida on gravel side roads, through the northern Everglades, and eventually skirting large, shallow Lake Okeechobee. The drive takes us through prime habitat for the snail kite, so we drive slowly and keep our eyes to the skies and telephone poles. We see some very cool birds— crested caracara, limpkin, roseate spoonbill, red-shouldered hawk, and more wood storks—but we don't see a snail kite. Or, at least, we don't see a bird we can unequivocally confirm as a snail kite.

The Everglades is our turnaround point. Although we once thought we might drive all the way out to Key West, we are now eager to flee the heat. And although it is too early for such thoughts, I can't restrain myself from thinking about home. We've been on the road for ten weeks, and we have to be home in six weeks or less. But there is still a lot to see between here at stifling Lake Okeechobee and beautiful British Columbia.

THIRTEEN

the eastern
SEABOARD

"The battle to feed all of humanity is over.
In the 1970s and 1980s hundreds of
millions of people will starve to death in spite
of any crash programs embarked upon now.
At this late date nothing can prevent a
substantial increase in the world death rate."
PAUL EHRLICH, *The Population Bomb*

Technology failed us on this trip, or perhaps we failed it.
Although we didn't get a GPS for the trip, we thought we would
be connected to the Internet almost every day. My hope was
that either Briana or I would do some quick research every
day—Googling interesting facts about our route, finding cool
locations to explore, and booking accommodations. Before
our departure, we had neither the time nor the organizational
skills to plan the trip in great detail, plus we were leery of over-
planning a route, knowing full well that we would soon deviate
from whatever route we picked. With the kids along, we really
wanted to take the trip one day at a time.

Our hopes for surfing the Internet while on the road hinged on our ageing laptop and a USB stick that we purchased from T-Mobile in Oregon. The USB stick was supposed to basically turn our laptop into a smartphone and allow access to the Internet from pretty much anywhere in the United States; in reality, it only worked in urban areas. When we were driving across Nevada or camped in rural Tennessee, the likelihood of having any Internet access was zero.

Why, you ask, didn't we just get a smartphone? Well, we couldn't find one in Canada that allowed us to surf south of the border without spending a veritable fortune on roaming fees—it seems we are still a few years away from true continent-wide connectivity. So we roamed across the whole continent without roaming at all. The limited Internet access had only been an occasional annoyance thus far, but now we were heading into the most congested region in the United States at the height of the summer holiday season. The ability to prebook campsites and identify the least painful route might be very useful.

Without prebooking anything, we head north. It takes us two days to get out of Florida, which is a bigger state than I previously imagined. Then we spend two nights in Savannah, Georgia, and one night in Charleston, South Carolina. Although our intention is to avoid cities, Briana is keen to see these southern cities, and they end up being the urban highlights of the trip. In particular, we love the city squares of Savannah, each one shaded by live oaks draped in Spanish moss. Briana and I could easily spend twenty-one days in Savannah, a day for each square, where we would read good books and sip lemonade. Such a trip will have to wait until we retire or find a good babysitter.

After Charleston, we stagger north through perhaps the hottest weather on a hot trip, 100 degrees Fahrenheit and unbearably humid. The southeast (really, the whole eastern half of the continent) is in the midst of one of the longest, most intense heat waves in living memory—it has hugged the whole region like a sweaty gorilla for the past three weeks. Even Ontario, my parents tell us via email, had an unbelievable humidex reading of 115 degrees Fahrenheit just yesterday. WTF?

Despite the heat, we go for a midday hike in Francis Marion National Forest. By 7 PM, we are looking for a nonexistent vacancy in Jacksonville, North Carolina. The local marine base, Camp Lejeune, is deploying a major combat unit to Afghanistan in a couple of days, and consequently, the soldiers' families from across the country are in town to see them off.

The seventeen-year-old girl working the front desk at the Motel 6 puts it bluntly, "'Tain't gonna be an empty room within a hundred miles of here." A quick check at two other motels indicates that she isn't exaggerating.

So, already exhausted, we brace ourselves for yet more driving. It takes us an hour to get to New Bern, where the motels are either full or outrageously overpriced. The one motel with vacancies is asking for $150 for a crappy $50 room, plus a $100 pet fee.

"You've got to be kidding me," I say.

"Take it or leave it," the grumpy man says. He looks strikingly like Roseanne Barr, so perhaps that is why he's so grumpy.

Finally, an hour and a half later, we find a vacancy at a crappy Econolodge in Washington, North Carolina.

"We've only got one room left," the nice man working the front desk says, "and unfortunately the air conditioner is broken."

I look at my watch and ask, "How much?"

"Fifty-nine bucks."

We open the door to the room, and the heat hits us as if we've just cracked the door on a pizza oven—an eyebrow-sizzling blast. The air temperature outside is still a sultry 90 degrees Fahrenheit, so the fact that hot air rushes out of the room is not a good sign. Inside the oven, I swear to God, it's 120 degrees Fahrenheit, a veritable Crock-Pot. Everything in the room is hot—Brora touches the TV and says "Hot!"

Everything in the room is covered in a fine layer of dust that suggests the room has been bottled up tight for a month. A piece of plywood is nailed across the opening in the wall where the air conditioner should be. Then, in the garbage can, I see some police tape crumpled into a ball, a wide yellow ribbon with "Police Line—Do Not Cross" written on it. I casually point it out to Briana.

"Great," she says. "Someone got murdered in this fucking furnace."

"Perhaps," I say, "a hooker just got beat up."

"I don't think they use police tape when there has been a minor assault," Briana says. "The hooker got shot."

"Or," I say, "the murderer simply shot the air conditioner and the hooker died of heat stroke."

Then we start laughing hysterically, because the whole situation is so horrible. The long drive, the heat, the bag of chips for dinner, the police tape, the presumably dead hooker.

"I can't believe," Briana says, "that you would subject your children to such abuse."

"Thank God," I say, "we just loaded up the cooler with ice and beer."

And with that, I strip down to my shorts and start chugging cold beer in the open doorway. A lot of alcohol, I decide, is going to be required to sleep tonight. Then I turn on the TV and scan desperately for cartoons—I need alcohol, but Brora needs cartoons or we will have a mutiny on our hands. Later, at like 1 AM, everyone is still awake and greasy with sweat, hooligans are skateboarding in the motel parking lot, and I am drunk—just another night in the Deep South.

In an attempt to circumvent congested Washington, D.C., and Baltimore, we head north along the coast to Norfolk, Virginia, and then cross the mouth of Chesapeake Bay on an impressive twenty-three-mile-long stretch of bridges and tunnels and artificial islands. Soon enough, we are out of Virginia and into Maryland, though only for a forty-mile stretch. Then we are in Delaware, a true blue state and north again of the Mason-Dixon line.

In Delaware, we drive through a series of nasty thunderstorms and emerge into a markedly cooler pocket of air, eighty degrees Fahrenheit and holding, which feels downright chilly. The thunderstorms have created a few campsite vacancies at Cape Henlopen State Park, and we reserve a spot for a couple of nights to give us a chance to relax and maybe see one of the handful of piping plovers that typically nest at Cape Henlopen. I've been fortunate to see piping plovers in Prince Edward Island, but that was more than a decade ago and I want to see one again.

Piping plovers (*Charadrius melodus*) are small, sparrow-sized shorebirds. They have sand-colored backs and lighter breasts, yellowish legs, and a black headband and necklace. They are perfectly camouflaged when sitting still on a sandy beach, and when they run, they run like a plover—run, stop, run, stop. They are globally endangered, with an estimated population size of perhaps five thousand pairs. Historically, piping plovers were often shot for the plume industry, which used the feathers of many now-endangered birds to decorate ladies' hats and such. More recently, piping plovers have declined because of habitat loss and general disturbance by humans. The problem is that piping plovers nest on sandy beaches, the same type of habitat that humans like to wreck with beach houses and off-road vehicles and bonfires and sandcastles. Many jurisdictions, from North Carolina to Newfoundland, now fence off sections of beach to limit human disturbance where piping plovers are nesting. Preventing beach access is always controversial, because there are so many people interested in using the beaches, and often the coastal tourism industry is based on good beach access.

The campsites at Cape Henlopen are packed a little tight, but the air temperature is perfect. Exhausted, we all crawl into the tent at eight o'clock and sleep like five dead dogs in the cool air. In the morning, I head out before dawn to look for a plover. I scan the beaches with the spotting scope for an hour, then I scan the dunes for an hour, and finally I scan a promising saltwater lagoon, but I can't find a piping plover anywhere. I return to the campsite for breakfast, and then we hike down the beach for a swim. The Atlantic is rough and cold, a stark contrast to the Gulf of Mexico, where we frolicked only a week ago.

That afternoon I chat up a park naturalist.

"There were only eight nesting pairs of piping plovers in Delaware this year," he says, "and now that the young have fledged, they can be hard to find. But we'll get a few fall migrants passing through before too long." His "fall migrants" comment startles me, because I can't believe that summer is waning and the fall migration will soon be upon us.

The next morning I repeat my piping plover search, refining my search areas after my discussion with the naturalist. I spend a full three hours at the saltwater lagoon and adjacent beach. But still I don't find a piping plover.

We take a midmorning ferry from Lewes, Delaware, to Cape May, New Jersey. Then we hop up the infamous Jersey Shore, stopping at a series of birding hot spots in an attempt to locate a piping plover. We start at Cape May Point, then the Cape May Migratory Bird Refuge, then several beaches along Delaware Bay, and finally Stone Harbor. At Stone Harbor, a small plover at a distance gets me excited, but the spotting scope clearly illuminates a semipalmated plover. That night, we are "lucky" to find a campsite at a private campground that offers little more than a patch of asphalt on which to pitch our tent. The campground is stuffed bumper to bumper with huge trailers, which give the impression of sausage links stuffed into a Styrofoam tray. We slide our little sausage into a tight space between a couple of rather dirty-looking links from Virginia and Ohio.

The next day, we try to circumnavigate New York City. We'd really like to stop for a few days in the Big Apple but decide that a separate trip will be required. A trip without a van or dog or even kids—a real adult trip.

The drive starts off smoothly. There's heavy traffic on the Garden State Parkway, but at least we're moving. Then, as we near the junction with 195, traffic stops dead. Ahead of us is a river of brake lights, seemingly a million cars bumper to bumper.

We sit there for more than an hour without moving. Then we creep along for one minute. Then we stop. Creep. Stop. Creep. Stop. Creep. Stop for good. The kids are awake and getting restless. Briana unbuckles and gets everyone a drink and a snack. Then she starts reading books. Then she leads a sing-along. Then she performs a puppet show with the ice scraper and a box of Kleenex.

"I'm dying here," she whispers to me in her Kleenex-box voice.

Then, suddenly, we are moving, and the entire van squeals with delight. Then the entire van groans as we come to a complete stop ten seconds later.

"This is what you get," I say in my grumpy voice, "when you pack 20 million people into one metropolitan area—a goddamn population bomb."

Although I was born after the publication of Paul Ehrlich's book *The Population Bomb*, it was a major influence on the early development of my environmental awareness. Even as a young teenager, the combination of exponential human growth and a finite planet seemed completely untenable to me. I'd not yet heard of the population bomb, but the notion was inherently obvious, even to someone with a grade-eight graphing ability. Then, in university, I read Ehrlich's book and similar books—*Small Is Beautiful, The End of Nature*—and I was convinced that overpopulation would soon be the major global threat.

In the early 1990s, when I was seriously depressed about a number of environmental issues, the human population growth curve still looked like an exponential growth curve. Predictions of 100 billion humans eventually roaming the planet were not uncommon. Thankfully, over the next twenty years, that exponential curve turned into a logistic curve, a curve that starts with an exponential bang but slows and finally stabilizes. Population data now suggest that the human population will peak at perhaps 11 billion or so, which is still a lot of mouths to feed but much more manageable than the 100 billion once predicted. After reaching its peak, it is expected that the human population will start to retract and eventually drop to some much smaller size.

The primary goal of conservation biology as a discipline is to get all species through this bottleneck of humanity with as much genetic diversity intact as possible. Then, in a few hundred years, when we hope there will be many fewer humans and a stronger environmental ethic, perhaps there will be enough wild space to allow most species to thrive without intensive intervention. In 1992, I truly thought that such an endpoint was unreachable, but now I am much more hopeful about the long-term prospects for North America's biodiversity, though neither the road trip nor my earlier experiences allow me any insight into the fate of biodiversity on other continents.

When you are stuck in a New York traffic jam, it is certainly hard to imagine that the population bomb has fizzled. Today, for instance, it ends up taking us nine hours to drive what Google Maps suggests should have taken only three. But much of the rest of the United States was emptier than I had envisioned before our departure. And, in some portions of the continent, significant rewilding is already occurring. If I have any hope for the planet, it hinges on the fact that Ehrlich ended up being overly gloomy with his predictions.

We wake in a motel on the outskirts of Hartford, Connecticut. Then we drive. Our only planned stop for the day is Walden Pond, on the outskirts of Concord, Massachusetts. Walden Pond is, of course, the pond on which Henry David Thoreau lived for two years while formalizing his environmental ethic. It is also where he started to write *Walden,* his environmental diatribe that was at least a century ahead of its time. For me, the book was another influential read, and therefore I wanted to picnic on the pond's shore and perhaps even swim in the pond that Thoreau drank from 164 years earlier.

We leave the highway in search of Walden Pond and immediately get lost. I had thought there would be more signage highlighting the route to the pond, but perhaps the signs have been removed now that everyone has GPS. Finally, after circling south of Concord for an hour, along lovely forested lanes, and then asking a nice cyclist to consult his smartphone, we find the right road through the forest. This whole area is a good example of a region that is rewilding; it is now significantly more forested than it was in Thoreau's day. The same could be said for most of the Eastern Seaboard, which is now more forested than at any point in the past two hundred years.

The road, however, is more parking lot than thoroughfare—the traffic along what should be a quiet country lane is bumper to bumper.

"Must be an accident," Briana says.

But it isn't an accident. The cars are waiting to access Walden Pond, not out of any interest in Thoreau but rather because it is a lovely summer day and the pond is the best swimming hole around. It takes twenty minutes to near the pond, and around noon we reach the entrance road only to see a sign that reads "Walden Pond closed. Will re-open at 5:30."

How can a pond be closed? I wonder. But then I see the throngs of people in Speedos desecrating what should be holy ground for the environmental movement.

"Let's get a picture of the damn pond," I say, "and get the hell out of here."

Briana jumps out of the van, runs across the road, and snaps a few pictures. Then we creep back toward the highway, which is now jammed with people heading north for the weekend.

We have a terrible time finding somewhere to stay along the coast. Every campsite is taken, and every motel is blazing a "No Vacancy" sign. The cities have emptied of their hordes, and everyone is heading up the coast. We end up spending $150 on a crappy motel, the most expensive room of our trip by $50. Then, for dinner, we have the option of crossing another endangered species off our list—a similarly overpriced Atlantic cod from the local fish restaurant. The Gulf of Maine still supports a modest Atlantic cod fishery, though like the Canadian fishery, it is now deemed to be in real trouble. We decide instead to cook pasta in our motel's parking lot.

We spend much of the following day frolicking on the beach at Reid State Park near Portland, Maine. The beaches and dunes are lovely, but we are also here to see a piping plover. With this goal in mind, I scan the beach with my binoculars from the comfort of our beach blanket. I don't see a plover, but I do see a man in the distance with his eye fixed to a spotting scope. I jog down the beach on a course to intercept. As I approach, I see that he is displaying all of the field marks of a serious birder—Leica scope, Leica binoculars, Tilley hat, Tilley pants, and Tilley vest.

This dude is a rare bird indeed, I think.

Concealing my comparatively crappy binoculars, I ask, "What have you got?"

"Piping plover," he says, without taking his eye from the scope. "Just one adult on the beach right now, but there was a fledgling here twenty minutes ago."

Following the line of his scope, I look through my binoculars and quickly find the distant plover foraging near the waterline.

"Take a look through the scope," he offers, stepping back.

Through the scope I can better see the bird's field marks— the plover bill and build, the single black necklace, and the black headband stretching eye to eye.

"We're driving up the coast," I say, "and I've been looking for one of these guys ever since Virginia."

"Well, you got lucky here," he says. "Only one pair nested here this summer."

We spend the night at a motel in Bangor, Maine. Although we don't know it at the time, this will be the last motel we stay in on the trip. Good campsites were much easier to find in Canada than they were on the Eastern Seaboard.

FOURTEEN

chumming for
A RIGHT WHALE

"Seasickness: at first you are
so sick you are afraid you will die,
and then you are so sick
you are afraid you won't die."
MARK TWAIN, *The Wit and Wisdom of Mark Twain*

The next morning, we cross back into Canada at the St. Stephen border crossing. The border crossing is practically deserted, the highway is empty, and the temperature is perfect—man, oh man, is it good to be back in quiet Canada after negotiating the throngs of humanity along the Eastern Seaboard.

That afternoon, we take the ferry to Grand Manan, an island off the coast of New Brunswick in the Bay of Fundy. We've picked Grand Manan as the main location for our East Coast adventure because it is reportedly one of the best spots to see critically endangered North Atlantic right whales.

The ferry, which is old and scheduled to be replaced at any minute, chugs for twenty miles across the lovely bay. We sit on the upper deck, watching the mainland slip away. Then, as we get farther into the bay, we see a number of interesting pelagic birds—northern gannet, greater shearwater, Wilson's storm petrel, red phalaropes, and razorbills. Then, finally, the cold wind sends us to the galley for perfect French fries and mugs of tea. The chairs inside are all lashed to the floor with rope, and there are Bibles aplenty to consult in times of need—clearly this stretch of water can get pretty nasty. But today the bay is calm, except for the swell that gently rolls the ferry side to side.

As we near the island, we see a number of whales spouting in the distance. We watch them through our binoculars and try to identify them using some reference material I printed out three and a half months earlier and miraculously found this morning while waiting for the ferry. The whales are huge, with curved dorsal fins—a member of the crew confirms my suspicions by telling us that they are fin whales, which are the second-largest whales in the world after only the blue whales.

Briana asks, "Aren't fin whales endangered too?"

"Yup," I say. "Almost every whale is still endangered to some extent."

We find the perfect campsite at Anchorage Provincial Park. Perfect for many reasons—our campsite is suitably private, only eight of the one hundred campsites are occupied, the washrooms would pass a naval inspection, and the beach is awesome. Perhaps it just feels perfect after negotiating the mad crowds of Ocean City, the Jersey Shore, New York City, Walden Pond, and Hampton Beach.

When I called ahead from the mainland to reserve a campsite, the lady chuckled. "I think you'll be just fine without reservations," she said.

"Grand Manan," I said to Briana after hanging up, "will be our kind of place."

We relax on the beach for our first full day on the island. On the second day, we go whale watching. To our disappointment, the North Atlantic right whales (*Eubalaena glacialis*) haven't shown up in the Grand Manan vicinity yet. The whale-watching company's biologist tells us that they haven't yet seen any right whales and that, for whatever reason, the whales have been delayed farther south, in the Gulf of Maine.

"There's lots and lots of finbacks and humpbacks," she says, "but no right whale so far."

"How about basking sharks?"

"Hopefully," she says. "We see one or two on most trips."

There are three species of right whale—the North Atlantic right whale, the North Pacific right whale, and the southern right whale. The southern species is reasonably secure, but both northern species are critically endangered. There are only about four hundred North Atlantic right whales and even fewer North Pacific right whales. A North Pacific right whale, for example, has not been seen in the waters of British Columbia for more than sixty years. All three species are similar in appearance—they are large-bodied baleen whales averaging about forty-seven feet long and 150,000 pounds. As a species, they are very recognizable because of the distinctive white patches or callosities on their heads. The callosities are strikingly white because they support large colonies of white whale lice, a parasitic crustacean. The male right whale is well known to have the largest testes, penis, and volume of ejaculate in the animal world—the testes typically weigh about 500 pounds, and the penis can be nine feet long. These enormous genitalia are coupled with a tiny brain, at least tiny relative to the whale's overall size, an anatomical combination that caused Canadian whale biologist Jon Lien to make the comment that "if the right whale thinks at all, we know what it is thinking about."

There is no mystery as to why the northern right whales declined dramatically and then almost disappeared. As is the case with almost all whales, the once-robust populations of right whales were devastated by whaling, first subsistence whaling and then commercial whaling. In fact, right whales are so named because they were considered the "right" whale to hunt—slow moving, coastal, heavily blubbered, and most important, known to float after being killed, allowing the blubber to be flensed from the carcass without having to haul the whale onto the whaling vessel. Right whales have been hunted by coastal communities for many centuries, and by 1800, they were already very scarce; it is hard to accurately estimate prewhaling population sizes of right whales because the whaling started so early. The Atlantic gray whale, which has been extinct for more than four hundred years and is known only from bones and historical accounts, did not survive this early subsistence hunting. (Remarkably, in 2010, a lone gray whale, presumably a wayward individual from the Pacific population, appeared off the coast of Israel. Could this be the start of recolonization?)

In 1937, an international agreement banned further harvest of North Atlantic right whales, though the agreement was regularly violated over the next few decades. The population in 1937 may have been as small as one hundred whales. Because of low reproductive rates and persistent threats, the species' recovery, if one can call it that, has been painfully slow. Although right whales have not recovered, many other species of whales have made substantial gains, thanks to the efforts of the International Whaling Commission, which has limited whaling since 1946 and banned almost all whaling since 1986. Along the west coast of North America, for example, gray whales have almost returned to preharvest levels. But two major threats to North Atlantic right whales remain: ship strikes and entanglement in commercial fishing gear, which together accounted for half of all mortalities over the past couple of decades.

We select a five-hour whale-watching tour that will take us out to the center of the mouth of the Bay of Fundy. The bay, which is best known for its huge tides, is also a very productive marine ecosystem; the mouth of the bay, in particular, is known to be a primary summer feeding ground for several species of whales and many species of seabird. The weather for our tour is perfect: sunny with a light breeze.

"What a great day to be on the ocean!" Briana exclaims.

Brora, more than a little unsure of the wobbly boat, jumps into my arms and remains there, screaming occasionally, for the rest of the trip.

The trip gets off to a promising start. Right away, almost in the harbor, a fin whale surfaces alongside the boat and offers fine views to everyone. Just beyond the whale, northern gannets are plunging into the water like feathered meteors. Then, only twenty minutes into the trip, we see the dorsal fin of a basking shark ominously cleaving the surface of the water.

Basking sharks (*Cetorhinus maximus*), typically more than twenty feet long, are the second-largest species of fish in the world, after the whale shark. Both the basking shark and whale shark are docile and make their living by passively straining plankton from the water, as baleen whales do, though they use modified gills to catch the plankton instead of baleen. Like the red grouper we ate in Florida and the Atlantic cod we almost ate in Maine, the basking shark is endangered solely because of commercial harvest, which is now typically only for its fins and oily liver. The shark is fully protected within the territorial waters of many nations, including Canada and the United States, but it is still taken in international waters and coastally in some areas. Our sighting of this basking shark is like a lot of marine sightings I've had—I find it hard to get any real sense of the animal from the deck of the boat. All we see is an isosceles triangle moving slowly through the water.

Soon after seeing the basking shark, we pull past the island and away from its protection. The swell and chop immediately increase, picking the boat up and then plopping it back down every few seconds. I take a deep breath, groan internally, and glance at my watch. My tendency to get seasick on all but the calmest of seas made my job as an at-sea observer a hellish nightmare—I took that job for a winter season in part to experience the romance of the open Pacific, but it is hard to feel anything close to romance with barf on your chin and the taste of bile always in your mouth.

We are an hour into the tour, still chugging toward the feeding grounds, when I realize Briana has turned grayish green.

"You've got to take Finn," she says.

I strap Finn into the carrier and hug Brora tight with one arm while Briana hangs precariously over the railing and deposits her morning oatmeal into the ocean. Mission accomplished, Briana lies down on the deck in a fetal position and abandons all attempts at parenting or whale watching.

Great, I think, looking at the kids and feeling my own bile rising, the next four hours are going to be some of the longest of my life.

My stomach survives until we get out to the feeding grounds. There we encounter a large number of whales, both fin and humpback. My adrenaline momentarily overcomes my seasickness, and I manage to take a bunch of pictures—the typical whale tail shots that litter postcards everywhere. Then the captain kills the engine and we start bobbing in the swell like a piece of flotsam. As long as we were underway, I was able to cling to my stomach contents with a gritty smile. But now, just bobbing there, front to back and side to side, I feel a wave of nausea rising up my esophagus. I look back toward land, hoping a steady horizon will steady my stomach, but there is no land to see—we have sailed over the horizon.

Shit, I wonder, how best to barf with two kids attached? Better not to lean over the railing, I decide.

I find the washroom below deck, but it is *ocupado*. I knock gently, wait thirty seconds, and knock again. No response. I knock louder, hammer with my fist, and finally kick the door repeatedly. When the door eventually opens, an elderly lady emerges, green as an elf.

"Sorry," I say. "I'm going to be sick."

"Go fuck yourself," she growls.

With barf literally in the back of my mouth, I can't even reciprocate the courtesy. I barge into the tiny bathroom, pin Brora to the wall with one leg and snug Finny tight into the carrier. Then I barf my guts out, stomach lining and all. I wash, rinse, and repeat the whole procedure two minutes later. Then I wash, rinse, and repeat the whole procedure three minutes later.

Thankfully, the kids seem relatively unfazed by the rough seas, though they are a little confused by their barfing father.

Fully purged, I stagger out of the bathroom and back up onto the deck, where Briana is turtled up into a ball, moaning like she has been kicked in the stomach by a mule.

"Oh, dear God," I hear her mumble, presumably to the Lord, "please let this end." Briana does not have a religious bone in her body, so I take the praying as an even clearer indication than the barfing that she is feeling truly terrible. I feel terrible, too, but I have a lot of experience with seasickness, and I am able to recover to some extent. At some point, I even start taking photos again. We don't get lucky and see the first right whales of the season, but the fins and humpbacks really put on quite a show. By the time we return to shore, Briana has recovered enough to be able to stumble off the boat without being carried.

"That was $300 well spent," I say, offering her a hand down the gangway.

The next day, we take the free ferry to White Head Island, a smaller adjacent island that offers some good beachcombing. The day after that, I overdose on some newly purchased Gravol and risk yet another whale-watching tour. Briana and the kids—no surprise—opt to relax at the beach. For this tour, I decide to go with a different tour company, but the outcome is almost identical. We see a lot of fins and humpbacks, but we also see a number of minke whales and Atlantic puffins, and I don't do any chumming. But we still don't see any right whales. In a week or two, the captain says, we should have some righties. But, of course, we can't wait around for another week or two. We're still 3,700 miles from home as a crow flies, and it is already July 29.

the long
ROAD HOME

"Literature and butterflies are the two
sweetest passions known to man."
VLADIMIR NABOKOV, *Radio Times*, October 1962

We spend six nights on Grand Manan, and we could have
stayed longer. It was easily the most relaxing stop on our trip,
except for the seasickness. After leaving the island and driving for three days, we arrive at Baie-Sainte-Catherine, where I
join yet another whale-watching tour with the goal of seeing
a few belugas. There is a chance I could see these whales from
a kayak or even from shore along the Saguenay River, but we
are starting to feel a little pressed for time, and I think a whale-
watching tour is my best bet.

Belugas (*Delphinapterus leucas*) are one of the most easily rec-
ognized animals on the planet—they are, of course, the white
whale. They are small for a whale—about thirteen feet long on
average—though some big males can be almost twenty feet
long. They have a very bulbous head, as a result of a fatty deposit

or "melon" on their foreheads. Belugas are an Arctic/subarctic species that occasionally strays farther south. The isolated population in the Saint Lawrence River, the one I am about to try to see, is the most southerly population in the world.

Belugas as a whole are reasonably numerous—perhaps 100,000 individuals roam over a very large geographic range. The overall numbers belie the beluga's fragility—the species is split into numerous populations, and some of these populations are quite endangered. The Saint Lawrence population, listed federally as threatened, is one example of a population that is still in trouble.

Trouble for the belugas began, not surprisingly, with whaling. Intensive commercial whaling, which started in the 1800s and persisted until the 1950s, reduced the population from more than ten thousand individuals to fewer than one thousand individuals. Post-whaling, the beluga population stopped declining but failed to rebound. Pollution has been suggested as one reason for the slow recovery; a lot of industrial effluent ends up in the Gulf of Saint Lawrence, and these toxins accumulate in the long-lived beluga to detrimental effect. Other factors that might inhibit their population growth include reduced food resources because of commercial fishing—belugas like to eat many of the same species that we like to eat—and general disturbance from human activities, such as whale watching.

And yet, here I am bombing across the choppy gulf in a zodiac, fueling demand for more zodiacs to recklessly ply this water. Fifteen minutes into the trip, our captain gets distracted by a fin whale. Then a breaching minke whale has us zooming across the mouth of the Saguenay. Next, the captain hears on the radio that a humpback is breaching, so we are suddenly zooming madly out into the gulf. The tour is only three hours long, and I am soon worried that with all of the whales around, we won't actually have the time to find some belugas. Another fin whale surfaces and we parallel it for five minutes as it repeatedly surfaces to get some oxygen. Then, much to my delight, the path of the fin whale intersects a pod of four belugas. We switch from paralleling the fin whale to paralleling the belugas for a few minutes, getting decent views and bad pictures before they finally dive into the depths. Then the captain hears something on the radio, and off we zoom.

Please let it be a blue whale, I say to myself, because the captain mentioned that one had been sighted a few days earlier. But it ends up being yet another fin whale.

We drive down the north shore of the Saint Lawrence to Quebec City, where we hope to spend the night in the old town, but we can't find a pet-friendly motel that doesn't cost more than Adie did. So, foiled,

Humpback whales

we camp on the outskirts in a tent parking lot. Nonetheless, we manage to spend a few hours in the city proper, sightseeing and eating two crepes apiece.

The next day, we cross the river and drive east to Montreal. Then, somewhat remorsefully, we turn south and cross the border into upstate New York. Just a little south of the border, we find a lovely campsite at Ausable Point State Park on Lake Champlain.

Why would we go out of our way to cross back into the United States? To try to find a Karner blue butterfly, of course.

In 1941, the Karner blue butterfly (*Lycaeides melissa samuelis*) was first scientifically described as a unique subspecies of the more numerous Melissa blue butterfly (*Lycaeides melissa*) by Vladimir Nabokov, distinguished lepidopterist and the author of *Lolita*, among many other books.

Karner blue butterfly

I have only trivial knowledge of both entomology and Nabokov, but I love that they collided on the outskirts of Albany, New York, resulting in the description of the Karner blue. I like to imagine Nabokov running around madly with his butterfly net all day and then changing gears in the evening to write one of the greatest novels of all time. Imagine the mind of Nabokov, capable of differentiating butterfly species based on the anatomical variation of their male genitalia and penning such magnificent prose.

Unlike Nabokov, I find entomology daunting: the diversity overwhelms me. For me, just getting to know a few of the 462 species of birds known to occur in Canada presents enough of a challenge. Insects are more diverse by orders of magnitude, and my brain simply doesn't have enough compartments. Sure, I can put most insects into the right order—a butterfly into Lepidoptera and a dragonfly into Odonata—and with some effort, I might be able to determine the right family. But, with much regret now, I have avoided delving any deeper into entomology.

The species list for our trip has similarly avoided proper treatment of endangered insects, relying unfairly on the Karner blue to represent the whole of Insecta. Given that insects account for 75 percent of all animals, and other invertebrates account for another 20 percent, the species list is embarrassingly biased toward vertebrates. That said, the conservation of invertebrates is still in its infancy, and in particular, the identification of the various subspecies, endangered or not, continues. The Karner blue is perhaps the most famous endangered insect in North America, and it has certainly attracted the most conservation dollars (more than many endangered vertebrates), so I thought it was a good insect to add to the list. Plus, there is the Nabokov angle, which is too cool.

Adie and I hit the road at 4:30 AM to begin the search for a Karner blue. From our campsite it is two hours south to the Karner blue habitat near Albany. The dubious plan is for me to drive down, find a Karner blue, and return to the campground before we are evicted from our campsite at 11 AM. Then we are somehow expected to arrive at my sister's house at 6 PM, in time for my dad's birthday party. I've Googled the route, and it can be done, but only if the butterfly and the traffic cooperate.

The drive south to Albany involves a quick stop at McDonald's for a coffee and two sausage McMuffins, one for me and one for Adie. So far on the trip, we've driven approximately thirteen thousand miles, and it is our very first bite of McDonald's—is this something to be proud of?

While driving and slurping the better-than-expected coffee, my thoughts turn somewhat surprisingly to teaching, the profession I will be returning to in short order. In particular, my thoughts turn to my lectures on the biodiversity crisis, the mass extinction of flora and fauna because of the many impacts of *Homo sapiens*. When lecturing about the biodiversity crisis to my first-year environmental studies students, I typically spend the better part of a two-hour lecture convincing my students we are in the midst of a major crisis. Convincing them isn't a particularly challenging task because these students are, not surprisingly, interested in environmental issues and nicely primed to hear the gospel of environmental doom. Toward the end of my diatribe, I show them a quote by E.O. Wilson, justifiably the most famous ecologist in the world, which states that "around 27,000 species are going extinct every year." I then ask the students if they think this quote is accurate, and they almost universally believe in its trueness despite not yet knowing E.O. Wilson from Adam. Then, rather nonchalantly, I ask them to get together in small groups and try to come up with the names of three species that have gone extinct in the past fifty years—the only stipulation is that they aren't allowed to access the Internet with their mobile devices.

Right away the good students are flustered. They, like most of us, are so used to going to the Internet for easy answers that they immediately feel like they've received a frontal lobotomy. They are also uncomfortably surprised by the fact that they can't immediately start listing off a long series of species that have recently gone extinct—they've just agreed to the notion that we are losing twenty-seven thousand species per year after all. Indeed, the entire class, brainstorming out loud, can rarely come up with even one species that has gone extinct in the past fifty years. Someone usually mentions the dodo and someone else mentions the passenger pigeon, but I inform them that these species went extinct in 1680 and 1914 respectively. Try the assignment yourself—it is not a trivial task.

If even those of us with a passion for the topic can't name even one species that has gone extinct in the past fifty years, how does E.O. Wilson come up with such a mind-boggling number of extinctions? His number, twenty-seven thousand extinctions per year, is not based on documented extinctions of named species; rather, it is a rough estimate of the number of unique species we are losing each year because of habitat loss. In simplest terms, Wilson determines how much habitat is being lost globally each year, and he then applies a mathematical formula called the species-area curve to estimate the number of unique species that would have resided in that amount of habitat. Isn't it depressing, I tell my students, that tens of thousands of species are going extinct each year that have not even been described by scientists yet.

But at this moment, while bombing south on 187 toward another endangered species, I find myself questioning E.O. Wilson's statistics, though I realize it is hard to question someone with the academic chops of E.O. Wilson, someone who is a real scientific hero to me. Perhaps I have always questioned his extinction numbers, and that is why I somewhat theatrically challenge my students to name a recently extinct species. If Wilson is correct, the planet would have lost well over half a million species since he first made his calculations in 1992, which is a lot of species indeed given only about 1.5 million species have so far been scientifically described. Of course, Wilson would argue that most species being lost are unnamed tropical insects and invertebrates. But if hundreds of thousands of invertebrates really have gone extinct with great rapidity, shouldn't the impacts of those vast losses of biodiversity have trickled up the trophic pyramid and resulted in the extinction of many hundreds of well-known birds and mammals? But here the data are quite clear—we haven't seen a plethora of vertebrate extinctions; over the last four centuries about 1.4 percent of birds and mammals have gone extinct, and the rate of extinction has actually slowed dramatically over the last five decades. So if the loss of all of those yet-to-be-described invertebrates is not affecting the rate of vertebrate extinctions, one could certainly argue that they are not particularly important from an ecological connection perspective or that the estimated number of extinctions is grossly inflated, as many critics of Wilson have suggested.

Unlike most of Wilson's critics, I do think every species deserves protection, but I also realize that the logistics of having a management plan for every invertebrate is simply unworkable. At the very least, each unique invertebrate would have to be identified, an immense task, and then population sizes and trends would also have to be determined, a much greater task. A more realistic goal is to continue doing what we have been doing: using vertebrate species as umbrella species (i.e., save enough habitat to save viable populations of each vertebrate species and assume that that amount of habitat will also be sufficient for the invertebrates). Although we could be doing a much better job of creating large umbrellas of habitat, I think this broad brush approach will typically be the best we can hope for. Designing and then implementing single species management plans for every non-vertebrate, except in rare cases such as the Karner blue or American chestnut, is simply not a viable option, monetarily or logistically.

I don't know why, at this moment on the empty 187, my thoughts have drifted to Wilson's numbers and my biodiversity lectures. Wilson probably intended his numbers to be more thought-provoking than accurate, but does such doom and gloom really further conservation biology as a discipline? In truth, few of our threatened environmental disasters have played out as predicted, and I can't help but think that these failed predictions weaken the public's belief in future environmental threats that, like climate change, might have real teeth. I also worry that I am losing the faith in the endless litany of environmental apocalypses, and I don't know what this will mean for my teaching. Will I be able to continue to preach the gospel of environmental decline with born-again passion if I no longer believe the scripture is as accurate as I once did? I guess I primarily want my students to be skeptical of pretty much everything, particularly skeptical of whatever I say but also skeptical of the calculations of the most famous ecologist in the world—perhaps skepticism is something to get passionate about.

I arrive in the hamlet of Wilton at 7 AM, right on schedule. But then I can't find the Wilton Wildlife Preserve, which is one of the only places in New York State where you can see a Karner blue. I don't have specific directions to the preserve, but I knew beforehand that Wilton was tiny, so I figured I could find the preserve easily enough. But after an hour of driving in concentric circles, I still can't find the preserve. Finally, I see a dog walker and ask him for directions to the preserve.

"You must be looking for a Karner blue," he says, and then provides perfect directions. My confusion stemmed from the fact that the town is on the west side of the highway, whereas the preserve is on the east side.

The main goal of the preserve, which is partly owned by the Nature Conservancy, is to provide suitable habitat for the Karner blue. The primary management technique for creating this habitat was to plant and then encourage fields of wild blue lupine, the sole food source for Karner blue larvae. The adults will sip nectar from a variety of flowers, but the caterpillars will only munch on lupine. Habitat loss and fire suppression are implicated in the loss of lupine meadows across the northeast, and as a result, the Karner blue's range has contracted to the point that the butterfly eventually became endangered. Controlled burns, which have been an important management technique for several species on our trip, are also important for maintaining the open habitat that allows the lupine, and thus the Karner blue, to thrive. Conservation biologists are only just becoming aware of the fact that it isn't enough to merely save habitat—often a monumental task—we also have to know how to appropriately disturb the habitat if we want to retain the full suite of native species.

I arrive at the preserve and hike out into the fields, flush with wildflowers in bloom. Right away, I see a number of monarch butterflies fluttering from flower to flower, but I don't see any Karner blues. I was expecting it to be an easy species to find; I had read online that thousands of individuals can be found in the preserve, and I thought I had timed my arrival nicely to coincide with the peak emergence of the second generation. I had even had a premonition of walking into the preserve and seeing a thousand little Karners blowing through the air like blue cherry blossoms.

But it was a false premonition. I run through the knee-high grasses for an hour, bloodying my bare shins and seeing a number of species of butterfly but nothing that remotely resembles a Karner blue. I peek at my watch nervously—it is already 9 AM, my turnaround time.

I zigzag through the field again. 9:20 AM. I zigzag through the field again. 9:40 AM. I zigzag through the field again. 10 AM. I am walking through the field and back to the van, completely downtrodden, when I see a flicker of blue.

I crouch down for a closer look, and there it is—a Karner blue, the most beautiful little butterfly I have ever seen. I watch it flutter around for a few minutes, snapping a few photos whenever it allows me to get close. I am watching this first butterfly flutter around when I see another blue take flight and stagger across the field.

"Thank you," I say to the blues. Then I run back to the van, late as shit for the party.

Weeks later, when discussing my Karner blue adventure with a friend and amateur entomologist, he tells me I should have looked for the Karner blues later in the day because many butterflies don't fly until the day warms up. And if they are not flying, a little butterfly like a Karner blue can be very hard to find. Perhaps shortly after I left the field, a thousand blues took flight.

I race back to the campsite like A.J. Foyt. Still, I arrive an hour and a half late—it is one of the few times on the trip that two cell phones really would have been useful. But Briana, as usual, is unfazed. She has packed down the campsite, fended off the warden, made sandwiches for the road, and worn the kids out at the beach. I load the gear and Briana loads the kids, and then we make a run for the border.

We arrive at the party just in time for cake. We eat the cake, and then we eat dinner. It is the first time in more than a decade that I have actually made it home for my father's birthday. We party late into the night, until at least eleven o'clock, and then we crash hard.

We spend seven more nights at my parents' house, rarely venturing beyond the property line. This visit is much more relaxing than the first. Despite the chaos, everyone, even my father, has found their groove. All the same concerns persist, but I recognize that everything will sort itself out in good time. Then, fully recuperated from our East Coast loop, we load the van with gear and kids and dog and wave good-bye. The image of my parents standing in the driveway waving good-bye triggers a lump in my throat the size of a grapefruit—what will transpire between now and whenever we see them again?

We only have two weeks to get home. The trick will be not to rush, to pace ourselves appropriately. The first day, we make it to Chutes Provincial Park west of Sudbury, where we watch the sunset while standing neck-deep in the river. The next day, we make it to Obatanga Provincial Park north of Wawa. We spend two nights at Obatanga because the weather is perfect, the campground is empty, and the boreal forest is in all of its August glory. The fourth day, we make it to Kakabeka Falls Provincial Park west of Thunder Bay.

By the fifth day, we have arrived in Manitoba and camp just across the border at Whiteshell Provincial Park. On day six of our Ontario-to-Vancouver leg, we cut south to Tolstoi, Manitoba, and have a picnic lunch at the Tall Grass Prairie Preserve east of town. Manitoba used to contain about 2,500 square miles of tall-grass prairie, but now less than 1 percent of that original acreage remains in a somewhat natural state, the rest having been plowed under for agriculture. Historically, tall-grass prairie formed the eastern edge of the Great Plains and Canadian Prairie, where soils were rich and rains more plentiful than farther west, where short-grass prairies dominated. Like so much endangered habitat we have travelled through, the tall-grass prairie ecosystem depends on fire for its maintenance and regeneration—fire burns back the encroaching forest and reduces exotic species.

The patch of tall grass that we pick for our picnic is one of the largest scraps left in Canada. After lunch, we walk a two-mile loop through the preserve on a trail bordered by grasses, grasses that are, not surprisingly, more than six feet tall. Halfway through the loop, we accidentally flush a pair of sandhill cranes with all of our squawking—the elegant four-foot-tall birds do a fair bit of squawking of their own as they fly away. That night, we camp at Turtle Mountain Provincial Park.

On day seven, we roll west through southern Saskatchewan on Highway 18, though "highway" is perhaps too robust of a word for this rough country road. I was hoping to see a whooping crane (*Grus americana*) in Saskatchewan, but I've called a few local birders and all of them suggest we are at least three weeks too early. The cranes, they say, will still be in Wood Buffalo National Park, which is the only breeding location of the last migratory population. Unfortunately, viewing the cranes on their breeding grounds is logistically impossible because they are so remote.

I'm not too fussed about missing the whooping cranes, though, since I've seen them before in the Aransas National Wildlife Refuge in Texas, which is where the cranes from Wood Buffalo spend the winter. That trip to Texas was, unbelievably, twenty years ago, when I was an undergrad. Rather than spend spring break partying in Daytona or studying at home, a few of us decided to take a birding trip to Texas. During the intervening twenty years, not much has changed for the whooping crane, which is still critically endangered, with perhaps only four hundred individuals in the wild. Persistent threats to the cranes are many—habitat loss, hurricanes, oil spills, oil sands, power lines, wind turbines, predators, and poachers—and extinction is still a very real possibility.

We are rolling down Highway 18, maybe an hour west of Estevan, when Briana swerves the van to avoid a roadkill.

"Stop!" I shout. "Turn around."

Briana looks at me and rolls her eyes, but she obliges me nonetheless. We pull onto the shoulder opposite the roadkill— even in its pancaked state, we can clearly identify the carcass as an American badger (*Taxidea taxus*). Sadly, it's the first wild badger I've ever seen.

I get out of the van and click a few pictures. In British Columbia and Ontario, different subspecies of badger are listed as endangered, but the prairie subspecies is supposedly quite plentiful.

That night, we make it to the eastern block of Grasslands National Park, where we camp under big prairie skies. Given that it is August, I was worried that the park would be busy, but as far as I can tell, we are the only people in the whole of the eastern block.

The next day, we drive a big loop around Grasslands National Park, from eastern block to western block. This corner of Saskatchewan, the southwestern corner, is practically devoid of people and basic services, and we come within a tablespoon of running out of gas.

After a stop for groceries in Val Marie, we head out into the western block for three nights of prairie goodness. We set up our tent on a ridge in the strong prairie wind, and again, we are completely alone—there isn't another person within eyeshot, and we can see a long way in every direction. We eat dinner and then we go for a walk across the prairie, through a black-tailed prairie dog town and down, eventually, to the muddy banks of the Frenchman River. In the far distance, we watch a herd of recently reintroduced plains bison grazing the open range like they are meant to. Then, walking along the river, we flush three white-tailed deer, all bachelors and all sporting fine racks. That night, the coyotes serenade us madly at close range.

In the morning, I wake at first light and again walk through the dog towns. I am hoping that I might see a swift fox or even a black-footed ferret, both species I failed to see in the wild on this trip. I see neither one, but it doesn't matter. For me, the trip has always been as much about habitat as species, and the habitat is beautiful.

Strolling in grasslands

Two days later, we leave Grasslands National Park and drive west on badly broken blacktop that finally accepts its fate and becomes a gravel road. Eventually, near Medicine Hat, Alberta, we rejoin the Trans-Canada Highway. That afternoon, we drive hard and make it all the way to Pincher Creek, Alberta, where we stay in a campground in the foothills west of town. Looking west, we can see snowcapped mountains surrounding the Crowsnest Pass. We can see British Columbia.

The next day we drive the Crowsnest Highway through southeastern British Columbia. West of Cranbrook, the police are controlling traffic around a serious accident. The charred remains in the ditch are a harsh reminder of just how lucky we have been on our trip. That night, eager to push on but too tired to do so safely, we camp near Rock Creek.

The next day, we descend into the Okanagan Valley. Then we climb up the backside of the Coast Mountains. We stop for a picnic lunch in E.C. Manning Provincial Park, where a late-August snow flurry sends us scurrying back to the van. Soon enough, we are descending into the floodplain of the Fraser River. Briana breathes deeply.

"I can smell the ocean," she says.

out of place
IN A WARMING WORLD

"Well, my son really loves wildlife.
And every time he draws a polar bear I want to
tell him there probably won't be any by the time...
he's my age. That's kinda hard to deal with."

THOM YORKE, lead singer of Radiohead,
Friends of the Earth interview, October 2007

After four months and sixteen thousand miles, the endangered species road trip still isn't finished. One species, the polar bear, remains on the list. But to see this species, I will temporarily have to abandon both vehicle and family: the minivan can't get me to polar bears, and the cost of getting to the bears necessitates solo travel. My plan is to fly to Churchill, Manitoba, for a few days of polar bear viewing—any longer and the amount of childcare I'd owe Briana would exceed my borrowing limit.

I fly from Vancouver to Winnipeg in early November and board a Calm Air flight to Churchill. Another way to go, and much cheaper, would be to take the VIA train from Winnipeg to Churchill, which is thirty-six hours each way and involves bisecting the entire girth of the Canadian Shield, from the Great Plains to the Hudson Bay Lowlands. This is the landscape of multiple Farley Mowat books, and I've been a fan since I first read *Lost in the Barrens* when I was ten. But again, I am pressed for time.

The flight leaves Winnipeg, and initially, the land below is carved into quarter sections, already harvested of their wheat or barley. Then we are over Lake Winnipeg, which is spotted with islands. On the far side of the lake, it's all black spruce and sphagnum moss—the threadbare soils of the boreal forest will clearly not tolerate a plow. For the rest of the way, the landscape below is more water than land, and even from the cruising altitude of the twin engine turbo prop, it looks difficult.

I land in Churchill with some trepidation. I have come to Churchill on my own, not with a tour group, which is how almost all tourists visit Churchill during the polar bear season. I simply can't afford the many thousands of dollars that are required to join one of these groups. But I'm not sure I would want to join one of these groups even if I could afford it—the images of tundra buggies, those 4x4 buses with giant tires and Plexiglassed viewing platforms, rolling up to habituated bears are somewhat horrifying. But if I don't join one of these groups, will I see a polar bear?

It is almost dark by the time I arrive at my bed and breakfast, Polar Bear B&B, which at $70 per night is less than a third of the cost of any motel in town during bear season, and it is more than adequate. At the local restaurant, Gypsy's Bakery, I ask a few locals if it is possible to see a polar bear without joining a tour group. Rent a truck, they advise, and drive down the road looking for bears like a local.

Ten minutes later, I am at Tamarack Rentals, where I am able to reserve a truck for the very next day. The cost is $90 a day plus fuel, which, if my math is correct, is substantially less than $5,000. Back at the B&B, I mention my plans to the young German staying in the room next to mine. "I must come with you!" he says, with wide-eyed excitement. I've met enough Germans in remote parts of Canada to know that there is nothing that will dissuade them when it comes to seeing wildlife.

"Be ready to go at eight," I say.

"I will be ready at seven," he replies.

Churchill is famous for polar bears (*Ursus maritimus*). By late October, they are congregating along the coast in anticipation of the Hudson Bay icing up, and Churchill is where the ice tends to form first. And after four months of nibbling occasional berries and goose eggs, the bears are eager to get back to eating ringed seals, which they can only catch when they are out on the ice.

There are approximately twenty-five thousand polar bears in the world, though because of the remoteness of their range, this is only a rough estimate. These bears are split among nineteen subpopulations, but there is enough movement between these subpopulations to keep the gene pool relatively homogenous. It would be hard, for example, to genetically differentiate a polar bear in Churchill from one, say, in Svalbard, Norway. The polar bear is listed as vulnerable by the International Union for Conservation of Nature, and in Canada it is listed as a species of concern. The polar bear's vulnerable status stems primarily from the expected long-term impacts of climate change on Arctic ecosystems, though hunting may be the more serious short-term threat for certain subpopulations. Of surprise to most people, overall polar bear population estimates have actually more than doubled over the past few decades, primarily as a result of tighter hunting restrictions.

The basics of climate change are now well entrenched in popular culture. The burning of fossil fuels releases carbon dioxide, and this carbon dioxide accumulates in the atmosphere, trapping heat like a blanket. The more fossil fuels we burn, the more carbon dioxide we release, the thicker the blanket grows, and the warmer the planet gets. If this warming is too great, or too fast, species will have trouble adapting to the changes. In particular, those species that are endangered or live in the high Arctic could get squeezed into extinction—endangered species because they often lack the evolutionary potential to evolve as the environment changes and high Arctic species because they can't move farther north in response to the warming. High Arctic species, particularly the polar bear, have become flagship species for many environmental organizations interested in funding their fight against climate change. Flagship species are those species—typically charismatic megafauna such as whales, tigers, and polar bears—that can be used to leverage more support for an environmental cause. The World Wildlife Fund has, for example, successfully used the panda as a flagship species to secure funding for a wide variety of conservation projects.

My own thoughts on climate change, for what they are worth, are a little complicated. I am very comfortable with the data that suggest the planet's climate has warmed significantly over the past fifty years and that this warming has accelerated over the past two decades. The shrinking of a large percentage of the planet's glaciers provides clear evidence that is easy to see and interpret. I am also comfortable with the notion that humans have contributed to this climate change through the burning of fossil fuels and habitat modification. How could we have burned the quantities of fossil fuels we have burned and modified the amount of habitat we have modified and not have had some impact on global climate?

That said, I am still leery of long-term climate predictions, the computer-generated datasets that forecast magical thresholds beyond which planetary doom will be inevitable. Predictive mathematical modeling of this sort is always sketchy, whether the model is designed to generate a two-week weather forecast, predict the severity of the upcoming winter, or estimate future returns of sockeye salmon. And there is nothing more daunting to accurately model than global climate.

All of this—the data to date and the future predictions— leaves me cautious about climate change. I am convinced that humans are having an impact on climate, but skeptical of the doom-and-gloom predictions associated with long-term climate modeling. Nevertheless, I think the global community should be fighting climate change, even taking radical measures. But I believe we should be fighting climate change in a way that makes sense even if the doom-and-gloom predictions turn out to be overblown. For example, if the global community is going to spend billions or even trillions fighting climate change and the options are to either build hypothetical machines that sequester carbon or build better public transit, I am much keener on better public transit. That mitigation will make perfect sense, regardless of how the empirical climate data play out. I also really don't want humans to have control over the planetary thermostat, sequestering and releasing carbon dioxide in an attempt to maintain climate stasis when climate stasis is anything but natural. And trillions of dollars could secure a vast amount of habitat for preservation, an expenditure that would likely have much greater benefits for global biodiversity than carbon management.

So will the polar bear really be extinct in the wild in thirty or forty years as some environmentalists predict? Over that time frame, there is likely to be a retraction of the geographic range of the polar bear—surely not a good thing—but certainly not outright extinction. The current range of the polar bear is truly vast. The Churchill bears, for example, are closer to the Mexican border than they are to the North Pole, so there is a lot of potential polar bear real estate to accommodate some range retraction. A more realistic question is whether there will still be polar bears in Manitoba and Ontario in thirty or forty years. Given that these subpopulations, the Western Hudson Bay and Southern Hudson Bay subpopulations, are at the southern limit of the polar bear's range, it is quite likely that they will be lost over the next few decades if climate models are accurate.

Although there is no road access to Churchill from the south, there are perhaps forty miles of road around Churchill, most of it rough gravel and most of it owing its existence to Churchill's military history—both Canada and the United States had a significant military presence here during the Cold War. From a polar bear perspective, the most important stretch of road is the twenty miles that skirts Hudson Bay from Cape Merry to the edge of Wapusk National Park. By eight o'clock the next morning we—the German and I—are halfway down this road, vast Hudson Bay on our left and scrubby subarctic forest on our right. As we bounce down the washboard road, we have a real sense of adventure. Neither of us has ever seen a polar bear in the wild.

Polar bears are big, dangerous bears. You'd rather meet a grizzly close up than a polar bear. Grizzlies typically eat grass, but polar bears typically eat seals the size of grizzlies. Consequently, to survive long in Churchill, you need to take bear safety very seriously. From a tourist's perspective, this means not walking anywhere outside of the town—even in town, a bear could pop up anywhere, but at least in town you've got the very well-armed citizenry close at hand. If you are outside of town, stay in or very close to your vehicle. Walking willy-nilly through the tundra or down a beach is seriously foolish. This is a drag for those of us who want our wildlife sightings not to be from a vehicle, but the reality is that trying to see a polar bear in the wild requires a great deal of caution.

Polar bear

The weary Arctic sun has barely crested the horizon when we see our first bear trotting right down the road toward us. We stop the truck on the right shoulder, and the bear stops on the left shoulder. I roll down my window—I am in the passenger seat because I have the better camera—and I start clicking photos. Then the bear walks slowly across the road and right in front of us and then alongside the truck. Not wanting to be the first person ever grabbed from a vehicle, I quickly roll my window back up. Then, indifferent, the bear ambles slowly off across the tundra. *Wunderbar! Wunderbar!*

We drive to the end of the road without seeing another bear. Then we start driving slowly back toward Churchill, but this time, we explore every scrappy side road. One side road terminates on a ridge near the bay that offers fine views in every direction. After scanning the local vicinity for bears, I get out and set up my spotting scope and slowly scan the landscape. In the distance, I see two bears, one huge and both moving slowly

Polar bear

through the tundra. We spend an hour there, watching these bears be bears, while keeping vigilant about our surroundings. It is the bear that you don't see that will cause you trouble. We can also see a few giant tundra buses in the distance, and it is clear they are doing exactly what we are doing— driving around and looking for bears.

We move to another location, a real hot spot, where we can simultaneously see five bears from the truck. Two of the bears spar for a minute; another stands to watch. The other two bears are sleeping in the willows. We drive in a little closer in hopes of getting some better photos, stopping as soon as one of the bears looks our way and sniffs. Like responsible wildlife viewing anywhere, responsible polar bear viewing means that not only are you safe but you also disturb the bears as little as possible. If a bear is responding to you, you are too close.

We continue all the way to Cape Merry, the end of the road and a national historic site. A Parks Canada interpreter, carrying a shotgun over his shoulder, accompanies us out to the old cannon battery. Across the Churchill River is the massive bulk of the Prince of Wales Fort, which was an important Hudson's Bay Company trading post in the 1700s.

"There's a bear swimming across the river," the interpreter says, pointing. The bear's white head is barely visible among the whitecaps that dot the big river. "You should come back in summer," he says. "In late June or early July, there are a few thousand belugas here and awesome birds."

By the end of the day, we have seen sixteen bears, as many as or more than they are seeing on the organized tours. We retire to the Seaport Hotel for beers and more beers. *Prost!*

The next day, I repeat the tour of Churchill without my young German friend—presumably hungover, he missed our scheduled departure time. The results of the second day are similar to those of the first, with lots of bears looking longingly at Hudson Bay in hopes of ice and seals. It's November 6 and the ice is still, seemingly, a couple of weeks away from forming. Historically, the bay would typically be solid ice by now, and the bears, if lucky, would be eating seal.

For how long each year, I wonder, can the bay remain ice-free and still support a population of polar bears?

epilogue

"Travel is glamorous only in retrospect."
PAUL THEROUX, in the *Washington Post*

Once we were home from the road trip, it didn't take long to get back to our previous workaday lives. Within a couple of weeks, Briana's maternity leave ended and I was back at the college. In mid-September—before I took my trip to Churchill—out of an odd sense of duty to complete the search for the endangered species on our list, I joined a whale-watching tour out of Victoria and saw killer whales (*Orcinus orca*), the endangered southern residents, from the bow of a zodiac. I'd seen them before from a kayak, which was obviously more satisfying, but my fatherly responsibilities necessitated a more pragmatic approach this time around.

For those interested in numbers, our road trip lasted 114 days, during which time we negotiated approximately sixteen thousand miles of North American roadway, including side trips. We spent a whopping $3,370 on fuel and traversed portions, sometimes slivers, of twenty-eight states and seven provinces. And, of course, we saw a lot of globally endangered species, including twenty-seven of the thirty-four species on our original species list, plus many other locally endangered species not discussed in this book. Most of the species on our list that we didn't see were species I didn't expect to see—ivory-billed woodpecker, jaguar, and Florida panther—but we also never saw a damn sage grouse or swift fox, despite expending significant effort in the search. This is undoubtedly a good thing, because it gives us a good excuse to return to southern Saskatchewan sooner rather than later in hopes of an encounter. If you happen to have a ranch house to rent for a season near Glentworth, Saskatchewan, please let me know.

Brora and Finn won't, of course, remember the trip, but I imagine that being in such intimate contact with both parents for twenty-four hours a day for four months will have had a lasting effect on their development, I hope positive. Both kids are fascinated by the pictures of the trip that now hang throughout our house, each image seeming to stir a vestigial memory. And we, the parents, will always remember the smallest details—howling coyotes, pancake breakfasts, swimming holes, roadside picnics, shimmering highways, dingy motels, and endless prairie skies.

Since returning from Churchill, I've been trying to synthesize a coherent opinion on the state of wildlife in North America. For what it is worth, I would now describe myself as moderately hopeful, despite the serious threats of climate change and continued habitat loss because of resource extraction. This hopefulness extends beyond the species on our list and includes a majority of terrestrial species and landscapes, though I remain gloomy about the future of marine systems as long as commercial fisheries continue unabated. Much of the doom and gloom I foresaw twenty years ago simply has not come to pass, though like a lot of young environmentalists, I was overly pessimistic, and now, like a lot of new parents, I am perhaps overly optimistic.

On our journey, I saw a continent that is in the midst of a modest rewilding as many habitats return to a more natural state. Large swaths of the continent are reforesting, apex predators are recolonizing significant portions of their historic ranges, and the population trends for many species of concern are positive. For example, most of the endangered species on our list are in much better shape than they were forty years ago, and I expect these trends to continue over the next thirty years. I realize this optimism puts me at odds with most environmentalists, and I am happy for our opinions to differ. Environmental advocacy, often fueled by a litany of depressing predictions, has been instrumental in helping to protect our shared environmental heritage. I hope the tenacity of young environmentalists continues to increase amid all the rewilding.

I'll end with a bold wager. When we repeat this journey in thirty years, as is our hope, I'll bet that the population estimates for all of the endangered species on our list, excluding only the spotted owl, will be higher than they are currently. I really hope I am right.

acknowledgments

This book covers a lot of geography and consequently owes its existence to many individuals. First, thanks to the many professional biologists and amateur naturalists who have helped to save both the species and spaces mentioned in these pages—many of them were kind enough to show me their study subjects in person or provide a little insider information via email.

Langara College supported both the road trip and subsequent book writing. The college generously funded a teaching leave, without which such an extensive road trip would have been impossible. The college's research committee also provided some needed road-trip funding. The Biology Department kindly hired and rescheduled in my absence.

Greystone Books, the finest of Canadian institutions, took a chance on yet another inexperienced writer, providing both financial and moral support for the project. Nancy Flight expertly edited the manuscript and deserves much credit for its final form. Dick Cannings, a superb writer and one of Canada's best naturalists, was kind enough to recommend the book idea to the folks at Greystone.

I am also grateful to Briana Fraser and Carmen Wittmeier for providing insightful comments on all aspects of the manuscript, and to Briana Fraser and Barb Gass for helping with the pre-trip research. Takuhiro Someya and Sean Kaczanowski expertly cared for our house, cats, and gardens while we were on the road. Lastly, and above all, my profoundest thanks to my intrepid family. Despite wanting to go to the south of France, Briana willingly embarked on a dubious road trip that spanned much of her maternity leave. Brora and Finn didn't have a choice about their road trip participation, but it was a true parental pleasure to watch them blossom in every landscape.